Advance Praise for

My Dark Nigh
Encounters with God

"This deeply personal, stunningly honest portrayal of Don Mitchell's experiences offers the reader a very explicit, contemporary example of the Dark Night. From its descriptions of searing purifications that progressively stretch the soul's capacity for God to its witness to life-changing transformations, these experiences ring true to the teaching of John of the Cross. Above all, they testify, as John does, to the possibility and wonder of a life of love lived in deep communion with Jesus Christ. In our sad time, the healing of emotional disconnectedness, the letting go of inner barriers, the movement toward deeper solidarity with those persons who are suffering are marks of this union we need to cherish. They open one's heart to enfold the collective grief of humanity with compassion, healing, and hope. Mitchell's experience holds out the promise of such a transformation of consciousness."

—Constance FitzGerald, O.C.D.

Baltimore Carmel

"The experience of the 'Dark Night' constitutes a crucial passage in the spiritual doctrine of the Christian tradition: the 'Passover' into the Bosom of God within the soul. The Dark Night, about which Chiara Lubich speaks, lived in union with Jesus Forsaken is a luminous testimony of this passage by Donald Mitchell. His pages on such Dark Nights tell of his intense life of encounter with God. These pages are enlightened by the experience of passing through Dark Nights to obtain the 'fruits of the Holy Spirit' that contributed to his work in the Church's dialogue with the great religious traditions of humanity."

—Fr. Piero Coda

Sophia University Institute

The Vatican's International Theological Commission

"At long last, we have in this intriguing volume containing a Catholic lay-person's detailed account of his own authentic experiences of the Dark Night of the Senses and the Dark Night of the Spirit. Don Mitchell invites the 21st-century reader into his own purifying and transforming journey, the fundamental contours of which were classically described by St. John of the Cross and St. Teresa of Avila. This Jesuit took special delight in witnessing a brother Jesuit's expert accompaniment of the author as he moved from discursive prayer into the new and mysterious waters of unitive prayer."

——Brian O. McDermott, S.J., Dr. Theol.
Georgetown University

My Dark Nights
Encounters with God

Keith F Egan

Dear Keith,
Thank you so much for guiding me in writing this book. It has a few typos in this first printing but the readers can understand + learn its Uno, Don

My Dark Nights

Encounters with God

DONALD W. MITCHELL

A Herder & Herder Book
THE CROSSROAD PUBLISHING COMPANY
NEW YORK

A Herder & Herder Book
The Crossroad Publishing Company www.crossroadpublishing.com

The text of this book is set in 12/16 Sabon LT Pro.

Composition by Rachel Dlugos
Cover design by Sophie Appel

Library of Congress Cataloging-in-Publication Data
available upon request from the Library of Congress.

ISBN 978-0-8245-8901-1 paperback
ISBN 978-0-8245-0364-2 cloth
ISBN 978-0-8245-0365-9 ePub
ISBN 978-0-8245-0366-6 mobi

Books published by The Crossroad Publishing Company may be purchased at special quantity discount rates for classes and institutional use. For information, please e-mail sales@crossroadpublishing.com.

For
Ann Mitchell
Whom God gave me as my wife
To bring me into the Church and to
Accompany me with her love, support,
And forgiveness for the past 53 years

CHAPTER 1

Dark Nights

Each person is unique. So, the experience of encounters with God in Dark Nights is different for each person given his or her personhood, life conditions, and the will of God for the person. There are similarities, but all Nights are not the same. St. John of the Cross's profound writings about what he terms the "dark night of sense" and the "dark night of the spirit" describe in great detail his Carmelite experiences of encounter with God's enlightening and purifying grace and the transformation it produced. Many of the spiritually rich and profound comments he makes about the actual processes and outcomes of the two Nights are common to all Dark Night journeys and can provide insights to those going through their own unique Dark Nights designed by God just for them. So, while I draw on St. John's guidance, my Dark Nights brought about the specific purifications, insights, and blessings by God's loving and transforming presence that God desired for me as a layperson and for His will for my life.

While each person is unique, he or she is also incomplete. Our uniqueness is given to us by God as a gift of Love. Our incompleteness is the result of the ups and especially the downs of the life we have lived that in different ways distorts the gift we are, our unique true self, and creates our false self. How can we become free from the distortions of our false self and discover our true self? John writes that the realization of our true self is not an achievement. It is the result of a healing grace that comes from God/Light/Love in the depths of our soul. With this healing, we discover God at the center of our being that brings the realization that "the entire universe is a sea of love in which [one's self] is engulfed, for conscious of the living point or center of love within oneself, one is unable to catch sight of the boundaries of this love." (LF 2.10)

John also says that this purification is like peeling back the skin of an onion. It is a slow "spiraling" process of healing in the depth of one's soul that eventually spirals out through our heart in caring for others and all of creation. What is at work in this process is an encounter with God's loving touch. But God is Light as well as Love. So, as this healing process takes place by the presence of God, His Light is so strong that it overwhelms the person's consciousness and he or she finds oneself in Darkness, a Dark Night. In this Night, one feels confusion and the pain due to the healing process. Yet, John says that "in the midst of these dark and loving afflictions, the soul feels a certain companionship and inner strength." (2N 11.7) As this Dark Night progresses, the layers of the false self are actually—and painfully—back until the true self with God at its center is revealed.

One very important aspect of this purification is the healing of memories. This too is painful since one remembers and relives the pain and its effects that has affected one over the years. But this healing is crucial since memories sink into the psyche as "roots" that affect our thoughts and emotions throughout our lives. To be able to live more freely in the "present moment," healing of memories is essential. (3A 5.7) Then, one can more freely believe, hope, and love with self-forgetfulness and self-giving. In fact, John even says, that, "A life of love of this purity is more precious to God, more precious for the soul, and more beneficial for the Church, even though it seems to be doing nothing, than all other works put together." (CB 29.2)

One thing that is very important to understand is that in the Dark Nights, God takes one beyond prayer and meditation to the gift of contemplation that arises from God. Prayer and meditation are what one does by oneself. Contemplation is a grace given by God. (2A 13.1–8, 1N 9.1–9) In the words of John, this contemplation is at its core "a secret and peaceful and loving inflow of God, which, if not hampered, fires the soul in the spirit of love." (1N 10.6) Also, God sometimes communicates contemplative images and thoughts during the Dark Nights. It is important to remember that in these Nights, God is always in control.

Finally, I refer to "Jesus Forsaken" many times in this book. John of the Cross writes about Jesus Forsaken: "At the moment of his death he was certainly annihilated in his soul, without any consolation or relief, since the Father left Him that way.... He was thereby compelled to cry out 'My God. My God. Why have you forsaken me?' (Mt. 27:46). This was the most extreme abandonment ... for He was forsaken by His Father ... so as to ... bring people to union with God." (2A 7.11)

My spirituality is that of the Focolare where we find Jesus Forsaken within ourselves and others. This is possible because Jesus on the Cross made Himself one with all who sin and suffer throughout history. He became one with all humankind in their sufferings, including each of us. Chiara Lubich, the founder of the Focolare, discovered the presence of Jesus Forsaken in her own suffering and the suffering of others. She discovered she could embrace Him both in between herself and others. Suffering became the space for her spiritual encounter and union with Jesus Forsaken. For us living Chiara's spirituality, this is also true. We embrace and love Him in our suffering and embrace and love Him in the suffering of others. Jesus Forsaken teaches us how to love others by making ourselves one with them as He did on the Cross.

CHAPTER 2

Prelude

It seems that God gives a person certain indications that a Dark Night is approaching. It is like evening time, and for me, that meant three things. First, certain events happened that indicated why it was necessary for me to make such a Night journey. For me, I began to recognize that there were particular things about myself that needed to be healed. This is itself painful to a degree because facing one's self with all its limitations, weaknesses, and woundedness is difficult. But the insight that comes with seeing the need for healing is that what needs to be healed are actually barriers to knowing and loving God.

Second, I felt afraid of the future. It reminded me of Jesus praying that the cup He was to drink be taken away. But He also prayed that God's will be done. This mix seemed to be the product of reason and grace. Reason and emotions told me that this path was not going to be anything I would choose. But grace seemed to be moving me forward at a depth level below what I could see happening to me. Third, I felt that while what was ahead was going to be difficult, I also felt that God would be with me. God would accompany me through the difficulties to a result that would be a positive change in myself and my life. I felt that God would be the actor in what was going to happen. God would be intimately involved in supporting me, guiding me, and healing me ... and that only by God's grace could His will for me take place.

In my case, the change began as my wife Ann and I were preparing ourselves and our three children for a sabbatical leave. Our preparation was during the Lenten Season when I seemed to be more and more aware of my "fallen" condition. This awareness was not just about myself, but about the world around me. On Ash Wednesday, I seemed to sense that "powers and principalities" move all our hearts to seek for what we want for ourselves, and not for God and His design for our lives. As I contemplated this picture, I felt that I add to this downward spiral ... that I participate in it. And even more upsetting, it participates in my distorting my life. So, I realized my need to change.

On Good Friday, I especially felt the heaviness of what Simone Weil calls "gravity" that was causing me to fall into the materialism of our secular society. For her, the opposite to this gravity is grace. Left to myself, I could not find a way to overcome this gravity and realized that I needed the grace of a loving God to rise up to a more spiritual life.

Then, during Mass the week after Easter, God seemed to catch my attention when a person took up the gifts to the altar. As he walked up the aisle, I had the impression that I was like the host being brought to the altar. I am a product of the earth, but I was being brought to the table of the Lord who alone can transform me. When the priest said, "Lift up your spirit," I felt mine being lifted up to the Lord who can sanctify it. Here is the grace that can overcome the gravity of my natural existence. I remembered Simone Veil's statement that the Cross that pushed Jesus down is the lever that raises us up. As I thought about this,

I began praying, "Come, Lord Jesus." But, I did not know what that would mean.

Later, on Ascension Thursday, I understood a bit more about what may be coming. The thing that struck me was when the disciples stood looking up at heaven after Jesus disappeared. Later, I wrote and prayed, "How tempting it is to hold onto Jesus. How can I let such a precious thing go? But maybe I need to find Him in a new way. I feel my experience of God is fainter now. God seems to be calling me to leave what relations I have with Jesus and find Him in a new way."

So, during the summer, Ann and I with Jimmy, David, and Kristy drove to Alfred, New York, for a Focolare retreat. We had become members of the Focolare and wanted to go to the summer retreat before going out to Berkeley, California, for a sabbatical leave. I was going to the Jesuit School of Theology in the Graduate Theological Union to study Christian spirituality. I had been a Buddhist before my conversion to the Catholic Church, and I wanted to participate in the new Buddhist-Christian dialogue in the area of spirituality. My friend and mentor, Fr. Raimondo Panikkar, suggested studying with the Jesuits. Also at the Graduate Theological Union were the Dominican and Franciscan Schools of Theology.

CHAPTER 3

Night Descends

When we arrived at the Mariapolis, I began to have physical and emotional problems that I would later learn were signs of the Dark Night. On Thursday night of the retreat, all of a sudden, I felt three distinct and sharp pains in my heart that sent physical tremors and waves of remorse and anxiety through my whole body. I had the sensation that I was being cut in pieces inside. At the same time, the retreat seemed to collapse around me, and I became very afraid. As Ann and I walked back to our dorm, I felt the desire to go to the rite of reconciliation. When we entered the hall where the priests were, I felt an immense pain in my soul that was so strong I thought I was going to die. So, I went to confession thinking this might be my final one. Afterward, I felt physically sick and exhausted as we returned to our dorm room. When I went to bed, something happened that I cannot really describe. All I can say is that I had terrible feelings and rolled in bed in agony and with a sense that all is meaningless. Eventually, the experience passed. But I was left with the sense I had lost everything. All the light, love, peace, joy, and faith were extinguished. I was left only with a sliver of love for Ann and my children. Night had fallen!

The next day was very difficult. At the final Mass of the retreat, I went to communion and gave my "nothing" to God. I felt that into that nothing, I received the Eucharist. I felt that Jesus was taking that nothingness and putting Himself crucified into it in some way I did not understand. But I felt that God was asking me to rely only on Him and to receive Him as often as possible in the Eucharist. I vowed to go to daily Mass the rest of my life, which I have done. Before leaving the Mariapolis and driving to California, I was sitting on a step behind the dorm. The person who introduced me to the Focolare, Adele Colella, was with me, and she too was suffering. We noticed two dead birds on the ground in front of us.

The Night continued as we drove to California. We stopped in Denver to visit Ann's sister and her family. I remember that while we were there, at times, the Darkness inside would be pierced by a ray of light/love from God. This ray would then fly out of me toward God. It was as if my desire for light and love was a thing inside me that split open the sky like a knife, and I felt for an instant the love of God. It was like the desire for God was itself the love of God. It was a glorious pain that made me cry and left me struck down by God's love. It only lasted a moment ... then, the heavens closed, and the Darkness returned.

I would add that it seemed that I was becoming more and more aware of suffering around me. It was as though God was using my own suffering as a window in my soul through which I could see more clearly and compassionately the suffering of others. Perhaps my pride was being broken down and I could identify with those in need in a new way. This was one aspect of what I experienced. The other was that in the suffering, I was beginning to recognize the face of Jesus Forsaken on the Cross.

He was there in my suffering and the suffering of others. And I could see more clearly why He said that what one does for the least, one does for Him.

CHAPTER 4

Night on Holy Hill

In early September, we arrived in San Francisco and took an apartment in Walnut Creek. We registered the kids for school and settled in. I went to the Graduate Theological Union (GTU) as a visiting scholar for the year. My home base was the Jesuit School of Theology (JST). The GTU is just up the hill from Berkeley campus, so it is called "Holy Hill." The person to whom I was assigned at the JST was Fr. Jake Empereur. I went to visit him in his office and in the conversation at one point shared my spiritual condition. Jake asked me a number of questions. Important to him seemed to be whether I could recall a "spiritual desolation" that began this condition. I shared about what happened at the Mariapolis ...but had no idea what a "desolation" was. He also used the word "consolation," which I also did not know what he meant, but it sounded better than a desolation.

Then, he asked me about my relationship with God prior to the desolation. I said that I had a close relation with God and the loss was very painful. He followed up by asking two questions. In my present state of desolation, was I always focusing on God as the central object of my concern? And, was I trying to do His will? I answered positive to both questions. He said that this was a good sign that a spiritual level of experience was involved and not just something psychological like depression. If I were just depressed, I would not have this deep care for God or for doing His will; I would not care about anything, nor would I want to do anything.

Finally, he asked me about my prayer life. Could I pray as I had in the past? I said that I could not. I could certainly say the words, but I could not "feel" anything. Also, the praying did not come from my heart as before. To pray made me agitated and left me feeling empty. Jake responded that this inability to pray as I had been doing was a sign that God had put aside the relationship we had before the desolation and was moving me toward a new kind of relationship. Since prayer reflects a relationship, Jake said that I would continue to feel very dry and empty. This being the case, he suggested I have a good spiritual director during this painful time of spiritual transition. He could not do it since spiritual direction was not his specialization. So, he suggested a few names and said that I should accept this passage and not look for the end of the process but just at the process itself with faith. "The process," he said, "will be difficult, but through it all, you are growing into a new and deeper relationship with God. So, do not fight the fear and pain, but accept and learn from it."

Jake concluded by saying things that sounded a bit scary. I could not follow what he was saying because he was using a spiritual vocabulary that I did not know. But I did think that if I could understand this vocabulary, I could perhaps make more sense of what I was experiencing. It was like I was entering a foreign territory with no map. On the other hand, I left the meeting thinking that God had led me to the right place for me to undergo what He had in mind for me.

A few days later, I attended a meeting of the faculty of the History of Spirituality Program. I was introduced to Fr. Michael

Buckley, Fr. Don Gelpi, and to Fr. Dan O'Hanlon. The students divided the Jesuits into "big ones" and "little ones." Michael, Don, and Dan were big ones, and I signed up for courses with all of them. The one with Michael was on John of the Cross, whom Jake had mentioned in our talk. Also, Dan was interested in Asian religions and offered a course on Thomas Merton. So, I chose him for my spiritual director. Don taught a course on the charisms and the sacraments.

CHAPTER 5

Spiritual Direction

Dan and I began to meet each week and discuss how I was feeling. Dan would then explain to me how I could begin to understand what was happening. The basic assumption seemed to be that below the emotional ups and downs, there was a spiritual process taking place that was moving me from one kind of relation with God to another. I needed to get in touch with this deeper process which he discerned to be a Dark Night. Taking Buckley's class on John of the Cross, I related what Dan had told me to John of the Cross's Dark Night of the Senses. In this Night, it seems to be an absence of God. However, the opposite is true. God is intensely at work in the person like a Light that is so bright that it is blinding. The Darkness is caused by the overwhelming Light of God deep inside myself.

The work of God in this Night is to withdraw all consolations of our senses, those that come from our life in the world as well as our consolations in prayer. This Night brings us to a new and deeper relation with God alone so that future consolations from God come from a deeper place within us, and we can do the will

14

of God that He has planned for us. So, this Night is the context for what John of the Cross calls a "passive purification" since I am not doing anything to make it happen. This purification makes one's senses dry and empty—that is, what one experiences through the senses has lost its effect on the person. But underneath, God brings one's faith and love to a new level in a deeper relation with God. At one point, Dan suggested that I might want to take a psychological approach to help me deal with the effects of this Night. But I felt that I needed to have a spiritual guide to help me with the spiritual issues as they arose. Dan agreed.

Given that decision, Dan gave me spiritual advice as to how to allow the spiritual process to develop while diminishing the more painful physical and emotional dimensions. One of the techniques that I found especially helpful is the following. When I would begin to feel overwhelmed by what was going on inside of me, I would gently yet firmly say, "No." Then, I would turn in prayer to God and entrust everything to His mercy. The idea here was to turn away from the fear to its opposite, trust in God. This moved the focus from the inner turmoil to God. The end of the journey was a new relationship with God, and I had to let the process take its time. If I focused on the painful effects of the process, I would forget the journey to God that is behind or below the psycho-emotional turmoil. Also, I could actually use the difficult and dark experience to turn more fully to God. I should add that this did not mean I could repress the painfulness on my emotional and psychological life. I accepted it but with my deeper consciousness turned to God.

When I was going through all this, I could not help but look at my weaknesses, failures, fears, temptations, limitations, etc. The point was not to dwell on them but as Dan said, "Let the thoughts and images arise into consciousness; look at them and then let them go by turning to the mercy of God." However, this was sometimes quite hard to do, especially when what was happening was fearful. So, Dan told me to remember what Ignatius said, namely, that the devil is like a barking dog who will leave if you stand your ground. But if you run, he will chase you. Or another metaphor that I found even more helpful: the dog is chained, and if you just keep walking, you will leave his neighborhood. Again, the idea is not to "get near" or focus on the fearful situation, but to keep moving eventually into the arms of God.

I should add at this point that since I really did not experience a presence of God to which I could turn, Dan suggested that I turn "in the direction of God even if He cannot be found in that direction." In other words, turn to prayer to God with the *faith* that He is there even if He seems to be absent. This will strengthen my faith in God even while sensing His absence. To this advice, I added what I had learned from the Focolare, namely, to embrace in faith Jesus Forsaken who on the Cross took on all the suffering crosses of humanity. That is, to believe that Jesus in His forsakenness took on everyone's, including my own, afflictions and sufferings.

Dan also emphasized that the attitude of detachment from the desolations should hold also for any consolations I might experience. For example, at times, I would feel an overwhelming desire to receive the Eucharist. This desire was not just a wishing to receive the Eucharist that I did not have available to me at the time. It as a deep experience of love for God whom I did not have with me at the time. It was a loving desire that moved out of my heart toward God. Sometimes, it was so strong that I felt that I could not move my body. If I was walking, I felt that I could not keep going. Then, as quickly as it came, the desire would pass. When something like that happens, Dan would say, just reflect on the experience for a moment, and then let it go. What you desire is not just a consolation from God, but the God of consolations. Put each experience, painful or divine, into the mercy of God.

Another point Dan made was based on a saying of St. Ignatius: "the devil is like a false lover who does not want his deeds disclosed to anyone. When they are disclosed, he runs away because then he knows he cannot succeed." This meant that I should share everything with my spiritual director. And that means especially things that I am tempted not to share. In fact, at times I felt the inclination not to share something with Dan, and when I finally did, it opened a new horizon in our discussion. And I found that whenever I did this, I felt relieved afterward like something was lifted from my shoulders.

Ignatius also said that the devil begins with suggesting something "good" and then leads us little by little into something bad. If we can retrace our steps backward from something we had fallen into, we can discern the negative progression. If we do that often enough, we can learn to catch ourselves more quickly and get hurt less often. This helped me to remember that just because something may be a good thing to do, it may not be the right thing to do. The good that God does not want is really bad in His eyes. Also, in discerning what to do in a certain situation, I learned that the decision should be made in peace. If I am upset about something, that distress will not be conducive to seeing clearly what the right thing to do is. So, if possible, I would wait until I felt at peace before making an important decision.

CHAPTER 6

Discernment

In applying Dan's advice, I began to learn a great deal about myself in a way that did not add to the suffering I was experiencing. Rather, I began to understand things about myself that helped me suffer less. To understand what was going on was a relief in itself. I remember thinking that it was like finding an oasis in the desert. You do not leave the desert, but are better able to live in it. And yet, given all of this, I also remember times when I was not sure Dan was right about what I was going through. It just seemed at times hard to believe I was actually going through something called a Dark Night.

On the other hand, there were times when I had to face the truth. For instance, Ignatius has rules for the discernment of spirits where he talks about the devil. On the other hand, at the GTU, it seemed popular to psychologize what Ignatius was saying in this regard. One Jesuit said that it was one's subconscious, not some external force that was involved. From my experience, it did seem that what I was in touch with at times was something "other" than just myself. Here are two examples taken from my journal written during a period of discernment:

Last Night, I awoke under terrible and fearful inner stress. It had the sensation of grinding or grating ... a kind of friction against my being as the feelings arose. It was like something going against me. As for the fear, it was not the feeling of being afraid. Rather, something else was mixed in with the fear that did not seem to be arise from me alone. It oppressed me in the fear. If I turned my attention to what was in the fear, it seemed to seek my total disintegration. I was led to horrible and negative and destructive feelings directed toward everything. So, I embraced Jesus Forsaken and turned my attention to Him. I found myself settling down into Him. This put the oppression into the background all around Jesus and myself. Then, there was not only a sense of affliction in the background, but brutal rage. However, I found peace with Jesus and did not let the commotion and noise disturb me. Eventually, it passed and I fell asleep. Later, I thought that below the surface, I was beginning to rest deeper in Christ ... but there is something that is trying to stop this passage into God from taking place.

One evening, I felt something enter into me. When I tried to read, I felt anxious like I should be doing something else. So, I went to bed. A loud noise in my head woke me up. I began to feel oppressed again. At the same time, I felt Jesus Forsaken as an almost soft presence within me. The affliction got stronger and stronger. But Jesus, though gentle, was stronger than the oppression. I focused on Jesus and prayed constantly the short prayer Dan taught me, "Passion of Christ, strengthen me!" I repeated this over and over like a mantra. Eventually, the oppression got so strong that all I could manage to say was "Jesus." But, I did feel His gentle and soft strength. What a difference between Jesus and the other force. Jesus is peaceful. The other is like a loud, strong, and noisy side show. The latter got so strong I felt like I was taken beyond the point of death. Death would be a relief. When I felt I could not live another second, the oppression broke suddenly and I relaxed, exhausted.

From these two experiences, I could see that there had been a progression from being confused and overwhelmed by the situations of this Dark Night to being able to discern the presence of Jesus—of Him Forsaken because on the Cross He took on all the sufferings of the world, including what I was suffering. I would add that through this process, I also gained a greater sensitivity to the evil force in the world. I came to experience more strongly Jesus's soft, gentle, mild, and peaceful presence while at the same time being a strong and immovable presence of God who is one with all the suffering people of the world. This opened my eyes and heart to a new and very deep compassion for suffering humanity... more than ever in my life. And, I also came to appreciate the years when I felt God's presence wrapping me in my loving family, in my church community, and in the Scriptures and the sacraments.

I was always able to draw on these gifts like spiritual water from the desert oasis for support during this Night journey. Ann and I and the kids became active members of our local church and the Focolare community in San Jose. Also, I went to daily Mass at the GTU and read the Scriptures—especially the Psalms—each day. My family was a great consolation to me. We explored San Francisco, Muir Woods, and the 16-mile drive down to Carmel. I felt that the unity I had in my family was essential to my health. It is also interesting that the children and our friends had no idea what was happening inside me. It did not affect them, which was a consolation.

A turning point in my journey was marked by an unusual experience. One day as I was walking home, I was thinking of some things we had been discussing about the sacraments in Don Gelpi's class. For some reason, I asked Jesus to teach me about these matters. Suddenly, I experienced something about the Eucharist that affected my whole self, my feelings, and even my body. It was an overwhelming experience of God's love for me! In that experience, I sensed that Jesus was talking to me. He told me something in that flash of light in the Darkness, namely, that He would rather I walk only in the Darkness of faith and trust in what I cannot see rather than seeking for moments when I can see.

That night, I felt afflicted again, but I also felt that my relation with Jesus had changed given His words to me. It seemed to me that I had reached a turning point in my journey. It was as if Jesus had taken me through a narrow crevice that grinded me because I was too big. It was like trying to enter the narrow gate while carrying a large load. But as Jesus pushed me through, the load was lightened. I felt as if I was somehow coming out the other side. I was emotionally drained and my body was weakened, but I also felt like I was now being "carried" by Jesus deeper into God.

Before going on to the next section, I want to share say something about Zen Buddhism, which I practiced for 10 years prior to my conversion to the Catholic Church. In Zen, there is a phenomenon called *makyo* that means "devil's world." This refers to a phenomenon that appears during Zen meditation at a crucial point before one gains *kensho*, or Zen Awakening. The scriptural tradition notes that the Buddha had this experience too. He called it "obstructing devils." The common form of *makyo* includes seeing or hearing things, feeling sensations, receiving revelations or insights, etc. These experiences affect the body and its movements. The types of *makyo* vary according to the personality and the history of the person.

In giving advice on how to deal with these kinds of unusual phenomena, Zen always stresses they can become obstacles to practice if one pays attention to them ... or becomes "ensnared" by them. Zen sees them as devoid of real religious significance. Therefore, one is always told to ignore makyo and turn one's attention back to one's practice with greater resolve. This advice seems a bit similar to that of Dan when he said that whatever the dog's barking may be, the important thing is to not pay attention and just keep walking. Whatever the experience may be, do not become attached to it.

CHAPTER 7

Contemplation

Some months later, the battle I had been experiencing within myself had passed to some extent, and a quieter period had begun. While the Darkness remained and there were still moments of pain and struggle, in general, times were more peaceful. Also, I had been praying each day according to the advice that Dan had given to me. With this change, Dan recommended that I follow the daily readings for the Mass. He said that by praying over the readings on which the whole Church was reflecting each day, I would feel less alone in my spiritual situation and more part of the Church as the Body of Christ. This would now be more possible given the peacefulness. In fact, I found this to be true. In the previous few months, I could only deal with what I experienced inside me.

The particular method Dan recommended was a modification of *Lectio Divina* of the Benedictines. It begins with *lectio* or reading the scriptural texts for the day. Then, if a passage, or line, or word moved my heart, I would reflect quietly on it in *meditatio* or meditation. If the meditation would deepen into an affective state, the, I would begin spontaneous prayer or *oratio*. Dan emphasized that at this point, I should be totally honest before God about what I thought or felt. I needed to bring myself in prayer just as I am before God. Even if I was afraid, angry, sad, or happy, I should be that way before God trusting in His love and acceptance of me just as I am. The last state of *Lectio Divina* is *contemplatio*, or contemplation. Contemplation is not something one does like reading, meditating. It is when God directly moves a person by an "infusion" of grace. In contemplation, one senses oneself being brought by God to a deep contemplative state. Dan said that I should not be concerned about this fourth stage. It is really God's concern, not mine.

Following this method, I often found myself in prayer just sitting peacefully with a new sense of inner stillness. It reminded me of deep Zen sitting. And just as the past afflictions seem to have had a source beyond myself, at times, so did this peacefulness. Sometimes, I felt that I was becoming peaceful and quiet. But other times, I was aware that I was being made peaceful and quiet—it was not something I did but something that was happening to me. It was in this latter kind of contemplative prayer brought about by God that led me to begin to find a new relationship with Him.

It was during this time that I shared something about my prayer life with a friend who was a nun. She reminded me of what St. Theresa of Avila said about the stages of prayer. There are two early forms of contemplation: the prayer of recollection and the prayer of quiet. The former is a gentler awareness of one's mind and senses being stilled for some time. The latter is stronger and lasts for a very short time. But it stills the body as well as the mind with a grace that seems to well up from inside oneself like an inner fountain. I told her that I could recognize the former but not the latter. She replied that it may come later, so do not try to force it.

As time went on, Dan reminded me of the old Chinese saying that if you try to catch a butterfly, it will always fly away. But if you stop trying, it will come and sit on your shoulder. Contemplation is freely given by God. If I try to get God to make my prayer "successful," it will fly away. God's time is not my time. I realized that behind my prayer was the desire to be successful. In the end, my prayer was motivated by spiritual pride—wanting to be perfect and trying to use God to achieve my own goal.

Dan pointed out that Christian perfection is love, and God can help a person grow in love in many different ways besides contemplation. The important thing is not to try to force something spiritual to happen. Rather, let whatever God wills for me to develop naturally and gently in God's own time. In other words, what God wills for me cannot be made to happen by some kind of "spiritual technique." So, I should just accept myself as I am. That is how God accepts me . . . just as I am. Do not try to escape from something you do not like about yourself. In prayer, be open to sharing with God who you are really, including your faults and mistakes, and place all in His hands. "Don't seek your own perfection in the spiritual life," Dan said. "Just seek God alone and He will take care of the rest in his own time and his own ways." Dan concluded by saying,

A spiritual journey is like being on a sightseeing bus. Just sit back and enjoy the trip as best you can. Play with your children; take care of yourself and Ann. Stop worrying so much and stop trying to change yourself. All that effort is like running ahead in the bus, trying to get to the destination sooner. Just accept who and where you are on the journey God is taking you. Trust in Him. There will be rough parts and smooth parts of the trip. God's grace

is always sufficient for you. After all, He is the driver of

the bus, not us. Just trust and relax and let Him take you

to the destination He has in mind for you in the way and

time that He wills in His infinite love for you.

After talking to Dan, I was better able to set myself aside and live more fully in the present moment with my family, friends, and fellow students at the GTU. Also, the Focolare Word of Life for that month was, "Whosoever loves his brother or sister lives in the light." (1 Jn: 2.10)

I found it interesting that when I let go of chasing butterflies, there were more moments of contemplative experiences during the day. It was like I had let the butterfly land on my still shoulder. Sometimes these contemplative experiences of encounter with God happened in prayer, but more often they seemed to happen out of the blue in the ordinariness of life. I realized that God indeed can do whatever He wants, whenever God wants. For example, one afternoon at the GTU, I felt very agitated and was just staring at the beautiful view of the bay from the window at the Dominican Center. Suddenly, I felt caught up into a peace and clarity in which I was frozen both in mind and body, totally focused on Jesus. I sat down after a while and felt like I was falling asleep in His arms. I wondered if God was beginning to introduce me more deeply to Jesus. In fact, this would eventually become clear.

Under Dan's direction, prayer continued to be a time of deeper peace and recollection for me. And as the weeks passed, there were two movements I could discern, or perhaps one movement with two dimensions. First, I felt I was moving in prayer deeper inside myself and even below myself. It was as if a door at the bottom of my consciousness opened by the grace of God and led me to a deeper place I had not known about from which I could pray in a new way. This place was not limited to myself, but was a depth that was greater than myself. In the deeper place, I seemed to be touching something more than myself. This "more" was paradoxically like a dynamic stillness lovingly embracing everything in creation. The effect was a sense of oneness with all of creation around me during the time I was not in prayer.

The second movement was related to this sense of "touching" more than myself. Actually, this more seemed to be touching me and raising me up to a new and more positive life. I sensed that this dynamic stillness, which is itself a paradox, was God. Also, I felt I was being emptied and filled at the same time. As I was being emptied, I was being filled with a greater relation to God. This new relation with God was like an inner oasis in my soul. I would add that for some reason, when I felt the need to pray as I had prayed in the past, I would flee from prayer at the slightest excuse. I also had the impression that God began to introduce me to certain realities about which I had not been aware. I felt that it was like finding rays of light in the Darkness. Or, it seemed that I was walking in a dark room and would bump into some object that God wanted me to find.

CHAPTER 8

Jesus Forsaken

Late one afternoon, our whole family was sightseeing in Carmel. We went to the mission, and in one of the rooms, there is a large statue of Mary. While in front of this statue, I had the impression that Jesus was giving Mary to me as my spiritual mother as he did with John at the foot of the Cross. It was not a big emotional experience. Rather, it was like an inner certainty that has with me remained unshaken. In the Focolare, we refer to Jesus Forsaken on the Cross and also Mary Desolate with Him nearby the Cross. I sensed that perhaps God wanted to introduce me more fully to them both.

One afternoon at the GTU, I felt disturbed and exhausted. So, I took a walk around the hills in Berkeley. It did not help, and I felt that something was going to erupt. Then, I was struck with the experience of Jesus accepting God's will, which is always love, and that entailed emptying Himself totally to be a channel of God's Love for humanity and all of creation. This was the passion of Jesus Forsaken on the Cross—to empty Himself to be a channel of God's love for humankind and creation. I knew this as a doctrine of faith, but in that moment, I could "see" the perfect love that is in His passion. But more than this, it seemed to me that this kenotic love of Jesus Forsaken was for everyone. That this love given as gift to us would in some way, I did not know how, crucify our ordinary false enclosed self that is formed by this world, in order to discover our true open self created by God. We are all called to break the shell we live in and let the inner seed of true life grow and blossom in living for others. This experience was so strong and challenging that I wrote the following:

Jesus Forsaken, You lived the height of Your passion for humankind and creation. You had experienced being united with Your Father as His Son in the Spirit of Love. But in this passion, You made Yourself one with us in our fall from unity with the Father. You gave back to the Father the Holy Spirit in which You were united to Him in Love, leaving Yourself absolutely empty, plunged into the darkness of abandonment! And yet, You still loved. You chose to say "Yes" to the Father at the same time You remained one with us in our darkness and suffering. You did this to be one with each of us in our pain— the pain of all humankind for all of history. What an immense passion of Love!

But after You died, You were not alone. You made Yourself one with all the suffering of humankind and nature to lovingly share our lives. You are Jesus Forsaken, my spouse. This is the highest mystery of divine Love. Only with the eyes of faith and the gift of grace can we see the mystery of this divine Love in Your passion culminating in the Cross. This is a grace that has moved me with a deep desire be one with You and Your love for each person and each living being.

It is important to note that a few days after this experience, I could not bring back this meaning of the Cross. It became a deep part of my faith. This was not uncommon according to Dan. He used the metaphor of a dark room. I have been in a dark room and now have bumped into a grace like an object that I felt for a moment and then lost it in the darkness. What remained was a faith in something I could no longer contact. Sometimes, I tried to reach out and cling to what I experienced. But it disintegrated in my hands. Dan said that if I thought I understood the Cross, it would not be the Cross ... so let it go and live what you understood in relation to others.

In fact, a few days later, God helped me see that this is something to be lived on our daily life. I would often sit under an olive tree near Gibbs Hall at the GTU. One day sitting there eating lunch and reading, I heard a child crying. It broke my peaceful silence. But, I was drawn to listen to the crying. It was as though it were Jesus crying in the child. It was the cry of Jesus Forsaken. He is one with the child crying. Suddenly, that crying seemed to be everywhere! I wrote:

The Buddhists are right when they say that everything is suffering. And we are all in ignorance of the Truth and treat others so badly, not even realizing this fact—delusion according to the Buddha. Jesus, it is You who cry out everywhere. It is You who is coming to me in suffering—my own and those around me. Now I hear You only with the ears of faith! It is as though in each suffering, You are giving Yourself to me to be embraced. I pray that God gives me the grace to embrace You in those who suffer, to kiss away the tears of a small child, in whom You are present. When I kiss the tears of the small child I am kissing Your tears. I see this, but to tell You the truth, it seems overwhelming to me. It boggles my mind and I am confused and afraid. I want to run away.

The smallness of my heart and the desire to run away became clear when I drove home. I saw Morgan, a neighbor boy of Kristy's age, lying in the street. He had been hit by a car and was crying for his mother. He was shaking with fear. Others had just arrived and were helping him. So, I parked my car and ran inside the house. I felt like God was making the point I had realized at Gibbs Hall. I understood that Jesus wanted me to embrace Him in Morgan here and now. I pulled myself together and went back to where Morgan and his mother were, and I helped cradle him until the police came. Then, I agreed to call his dad and keep his sister in our apartment while his mother went with him to the hospital.

This was the beginning of a series of similar experiences where it seemed that Jesus wanted me to find Him in the crosses of others. I sensed that God was showing me that we are called to be His hands in carrying the crosses of others, each of which contains the Cross of God's Son. But at the same time, I realized that there is a dark opposition to this way of life in the world. There is a rejection of the Cross, a rejection of God's presence in the suffering of humanity, and a rejection of God's call to each of us to minister to His Son in the suffering of humankind. Instead, so many people pursue the riches of the world and build a bubble around themselves to avoid the suffering of others. And in Morgan, I saw this in myself. I parked my car and went into our peaceful apartment to avoid dealing with a suffering child. Fear held me back in this case. But all around us, there are forces of spiritual gravity pulling us downward into indifference, avoidance, and then deeper into discrimination, prejudice, racism, antisemitism, etc. There is also greed pulling us above the sufferings of this world to be like the Greek gods isolated from human suffering, enjoying the pleasures of their riches. At one point, I wrote:

> The winds in the desert journey blow us around, up, and down. On all sides, one feels pushed by the winds of the desert in directions that lead deeper into a wasteland. But it is really a time for making the choice of God alone. It is a time for faith and trust in God alone, a time for hope in God alone, and a time to love God alone. God is the oasis of grace in the barren desert.

While I know this, and am coming to experience it more, I also am victim to the thoughts blowing through my mind, shaking me, and sometimes overwhelming me. Then, sometimes the desert winds stop and there I am back at the oasis, free and clear. This would happen especially when I received the Eucharist. But then, the winds would blow again, and my feelings would be dry and arid, sad and sick, anxious and lost. Then, the choice or God is alone before me. And each time I make this choice, God gives me Jesus in my sufferings and those of others around me. It seems more and more that it is to Jesus that God is leading me.

In discussing this with Dan, he said that he felt comfortable with my perception of the movement toward Jesus. To discover a deeper relationship with God in Jesus is an important step in the Night I have been in. Even if I sense Darkness, perhaps less as time goes on, this path is clearer for this Night. He cautioned me to be careful in this movement not to focus my attention on trying to understand more "things," new information. The journey is one of formation by God leading to Jesus.

At that time, I also spoke with Jim Connor, a Trappist monk who was assistant novice master with Thomas Merton. Dan thought it would be good to talk to him since he was visiting the GTU. Jim asked me a number of questions and then said that as I turn more to Jesus, I should rely on a "Dark Faith" in Jesus and trust in Him for everything. He said that my concentration on the things I had learned so far on the journey was a sign of my sincerity. But to continue, I need to open my hands for that what will come. He said that I was fortunate to be with the Jesuits for spiritual direction. God brought me to the right place. And, God will complete this journey in the right time—His time not mine.

CHAPTER 9

Jesus

S pring was coming to San Francisco earlier than it does in the Midwest. The hills have been brown, and now with the spring rains, they were turning dark green. At the same time, I felt something new was beginning to grow within me. I felt drawn to pray to Jesus, to focus on Jesus and His love for me. However, I did not know what that meant. Dan was away from campus, so I asked St. Joseph to help me since He contemplated Jesus for many years. What then happened when I then sat down to pray marked a new relationship with Jesus:

I followed the Ignatius's Exercises approach using my imagination. The first thought I had was the time when Joseph and Mary lost Jesus in the Temple. It seemed to me that I as the one who lost Jesus and was entering the Temple of God in my heart to find Him. There, I saw

Jesus talking with love to my heart. He was teaching my heart, but I could not hear what He was saying. I approached and sat down. When I sat, it seemed like I was a child looking at Him. He turned and said that He loves me and that He had been speaking "kind and gentle" words of love to my heart. "But," He said, "you are always distracted by what I say and do and do not look for Me." "But where do I find You, Lord? I have been looking for You all this time." He replied, "I have always been here. You are the one who wanders off looking at this or that. Instead, you should just sit down like you would with a small child you love, who wants to share something with you that she thinks is important." When Jesus spoke, He seemed like a child, gentle and soft, yet with such amazing wisdom and love that His words brought joy to my heart!

Jesus said that He was saying to my heart nothing more than the Truth in the Scriptures, but in doing so, He was "imprinting them in my heart." I understood that His words in the Scriptures are not just to be read, but are words of the Word to form our souls, our lives, with divine nourishment of the Truth. Thus, nourished, we can "do" the Truth from our transformed hearts with the gentleness of Jesus. We can do His will.

And as I step back, I think, perhaps this is the point of this whole Night: to enable me to do His will for me: to enter interreligious dialogue in a way that enables Jesus to speak from my heart, soft and gentle but with light of Truth that others can understand.

When I saw Dan after this experience, he told me that the insight was right when Jesus asked me to set aside the various "insights" I had, and focus on what God wants me to know at this time—Jesus. I was always looking at the consolations God was giving me, and not to the God of the consolations. I told Dan that since this experience, I was beginning to feel a new peace and strength. It did not develop slowly, but it was like waking up one morning and seeing a new blossom on a flower that you had not noticed before.

Dan said that my being drawn to the humanity of Jesus was good. As Teresa of Avila said, no matter what stage of the spiritual life one is at, there is always a need to focus on the person-hood of Jesus. He said, "As you put things in your life in a new order as a Christian, your relationship with Jesus should be at the center of this new order. Reading Jesus's words in the Gospels will help you."

At Christmas time, Dan's words seemed to be confirmed in my own experience. I had the clear impression that God was everywhere, the horizon of each present moment. However, as I realized this "fact" more and more, at the same time, I did not *feel* it. It was as though I realized the preciousness of all things experienced in God, and yet God felt as if He was not there. I understood God's presence behind and within all things, but only felt His absence.

Then, as time went on, it seemed as through God's infinite horizon had emptied itself into Jesus. I knew the divine horizon of God was there, but now I only *felt* its presence in Jesus. This experience seemed to me to be the meaning of Christmas—God born in Jesus Christ. It seemed as if God-Love rushed in from the horizon into Jesus in me and lifted me to a speechless joy and filled me with a deep calm—the joy and peace of Christmas!

As the Lenten season approached, I looked at the Stations of the Cross on the walls of the church we went to as a family. Growing up as a Protestant, I did not know much about them. Plus, at St. Tom's at Purdue where I went to Mass, the walls were bare in the style of a monastery. So, I picked up a booklet on the Stations of the Cross and used that for meditation. Here are my notes about each one:

1. "Jesus Condemned": What a great sorrow Mary must
    have felt! And how many mothers in this world experi-
    ence the condemnation of their children. And how many
    times do I condemn people, making their mothers weep?
    When I was in high school, I was sitting waiting for a
    city bus, and I saw a classmate run from the school to
    the street on his way home crying. I thought of what his
    mother would feel, and I cried too.

2. "Jesus taking up the Cross": He took up all our crosses, sins, and sufferings. From the wood of the Cross comes a fire that burns deeply in a secret place within us. The fire destroys the distance between us and God, so in each suffering, we are one with Jesus linking us with His Father. The cross we carry is still there, but God-Love is too. While the crosses may pass, Love remains. I imagined Jesus carrying the Cross that got bigger and bigger until it dwarfed the world from the beginning of time to the end.

3. "Jesus falls the first time": Jesus is human like us, and He stumbles and falls like us. So, in our stumbling, both physically and morally, He consoles us. We are like children who lose their way, or hurt themselves, or come down with an incurable illness. Jesus is there with us. God's mercy in Jesus is a warmth that embraces everything with a mother's tenderness.

4. "Jesus meets His mother": This is a very touching meditation. In some ways, it is beyond words. Yet it is a picture of Mary Desolate with Jesus Forsaken. When we suffer, we can find Jesus Forsaken within our suffering as Mary did. It seems to me that they are always together

embracing the suffering of all persons, perhaps all living beings. If we realize this embrace, we find not only the love of God for us, but the love of Mary that she has for her Son.

5. "Simon is forced to take up the Cross": The evil forces that oppose and oppress Jesus do the same with us. Jesus did not and does not force anyone to carry a cross; the world does. And when we have to carry a cross, we can meet Jesus who has taken that cross and made it part of His Cross. It is interesting that the man that the evil in the world chose to take up Jesus's Cross was named Simon, like Simon Peter. Perhaps that indicates the crosses that the Church has had to carry for 2,000 years.

6. "Veronica consoles Jesus": What a blessing to be consoled. What a grace it is to be able to console others and through them to console Jesus who is with them on their cross. It makes me realize how little my generosity and compassion is when it comes to consoling others. I hold back so much and need to step forward out of the crowd.

7. "The people press in on Jesus": They mock and scorn Him from their hate, and the weight of the Cross increases. His pain increases and He falls again. People

today are also pressed by those who do not understand them and reject them. This causes pain to the point that people fall. And sometimes we do this to ourselves.

8. "The women weeping for Jesus": Jesus says, "Weep for yourselves and your children." This may mean what will befall Jerusalem. But I think it means something for all humanity. How many times do we expect things to go well for ourselves and our children? But things just happen in this material world where nothing is perfect or suffering-proof. By the Cross He carries, Jesus will be one with all mothers, fathers, and children who suffer.

9. "Jesus bears the insults of the crowd": Today, people insult Jesus directly and also Jesus in their neighbors. Racism, antisemitism, ethnic hatred ... in so many ways today, people insult and injure Jesus in their neighbors. Jesus bears these attacks, sharing the pain and humiliation of all who suffer at the hands of others. "What you do to others you do to Me." We are called to stand up for and care for those who are victims of crowds.

10. "They take Jesus's clothes": Jesus shows us how to give up everything of this world in order to love others. Thomas Merton said that those who imagine themselves

blessed by God with money and do not share with others in need are the most wretched of people because they frustrate the will of God. Jesus held nothing back for the salvation of the world. His poverty was now complete, and in it He shows us how to give all to "Love others as I loved you."

11. "Jesus is nailed to the Cross": Jesus's most precious blood is poured out of His body. Blood represented life, so He pours out the life from His body as a gift for us. Jesus takes the painful burdens of our lives into His heart, and pours out of His sacred heart the blood of new life. Now it is also the wine in the Eucharist. Only God could do this! How much God loves us!

12. "Jesus dies." His disciples left Him except John whom He has given to his mother. His clothes are gone and He is stripped of all dignity. He even experiences abandonment by the Father. The divine *kenosis* of love is complete. But as His Cross was put into the ground, He is the seed that is put into the ground only to produce new life for all of us.

13. "Jesus dead is held in His mother's arms." A mother and her dead Son—no more pity can be found than this! It

is a divine moment. The *kenosis* of Jesus is complete; the self-emptying of God as an act of love for humanity is complete. And the *kenosis* of Mary is also complete. She has lost her Son and her God. Into the nothingness of Mary is poured the nothingness of Jesus. I believe that where there is Jesus Forsaken, there is always Mary Desolate.

14. "Jesus is buried": The seed is buried and will flower with new life—the risen Jesus. And in His mystical body, we are all one like fresh branches on the vine coming out of the ground.

After this time of meditation on the Stations of the Cross, at Mass I looked at the host and really felt it was the presence of Jesus. I thought, *This is truly God!* Then, I composed this child-like story:

A priest who was a bit absent-minded lost a consecrated host in his sleeve. As he walked to the rectory, it dropped on the ground. It eventually disintegrated into the ground for the winter. In the spring, a flower grew up in that spot nourished by the host. A little girl riding her tricycle came by, saw the flower and picked it to take home to her mother. Her mother put it on the table in a glass of water, and the fragrance filled the room. That night, the little girl fell asleep in an atmosphere of deep peace. She dreamed that an angel arose from the flower and told her about God's special love for her. The angel described how God created her with special love and care just the way she is. God would love her always. At breakfast, the little girl noticed that the flower had died during the night. But the message from the angel remained in her heart forever.

CHAPTER 10

God/Love in Jesus

My reaction to the experiences of encountering God/Love in Jesus was threefold. First, I found myself more and more able to entrust myself to Jesus as I understood the infinite depth and constancy of His love for me. The image I had was of a child leaping from a wall, knowing she will be caught by her loving parent. He said that we must become like little children. This did not mean He would remove all suffering from my life, but as Jesus Forsaken, He has already taken my sufferings from birth to death into His loving arms.

Second, I found this embrace by Jesus enabled me to accept myself with all my shortcomings, weaknesses, and wounds from the past. I saw that these were not barriers to God's love for me, but actually attracted God's love to me. Like a small child who makes mistakes and cannot do certain things, I am lovable too. And this relationship with Jesus at this new level of acceptance and oneness found as a Light in the Darkness enabled me to accept myself more fully with all my weaknesses and limitations. And it also meant that if God was calling me into dialogue with persons of other religions, God would give would be in my heart, so my dialogue could come from my heart where He has written the Truth.

Third, I felt more deeply that I can better love others as Jesus was loving me. This means setting aside judgment and accepting with compassion those who are seen as the least by society . . . the persons Jesus lists as those who we are to love in order to love Him. It also means that I must be empty of self and judgments of others and love each person as a brother or sister. Knowing now that God/Love is with me in Jesus, I felt that it is His strength in me that enables me to make myself one with those to suffer, to share their suffering, accepting them as they are . . . as He did for me.

Having said these three things, I was also aware that I was not heading to sainthood. My personality meant that these three things were ideals. And knowing myself, I will often fall short. In fact, I was also beginning to understand that God respected my freedom. Entrusting myself to a deeper relation with Jesus does not mean He is moving me toward perfection. God was not disburdening me from making decisions in living my life. Jesus was within me to support and care for me in a manner that respects my freedom. I need to walk on my own two feet, as it were; and this means I will always be making mistakes and taking wrong turns. In all, I must rely on the mercy of God. I thought about Dan's class on Thomas Merton when we read *The Sign of Jonah*. God told him to go and do something, and he went in the opposite direction. So, God had to turn him around in the belly of the fish. Being in a Dark Night is a bit like being in a fish's belly, a dark and cramped place. But, eventually, the fish spat Jonah out onto the land. Then, he was walking in the right direction … but he had to do the walking on his own two feet. And while he did what God asked, he had a hard time accepting God's decision to forgive. God has taken me into a cramped Night where I could not move, but I sensed that once this Night is over, I will be spit out of the Darkness to do God's will ... but I, like Jonah, will still be an imperfect human being. I have found God's presence and have begun by God's grace to form more deeply a Christian identity. It involves a relationship with Jesus, and I realize that this relationship will remain in my heart. That gives me hope.

Edward Malatesta once remarked in class that silent and formless prayer must be complemented by Scripture reading and reflection thereby on Jesus as a person. He said that it was important to let the mysteries of Jesus's life affect our lives in order to have a deeper Christian faith life. True Christian spiritual formation does not lead to perfection, but to a more intimate relationship with Jesus, even with our imperfections.

CHAPTER 11

Easter

With Ash Wednesday, my mood and my feelings began to change even more significantly. And as they did, I felt a sense of gladness and gratitude. As this change took place, I also felt more of an awareness of Jesus, especially at Mass. It was like a spring inside me bubbling up into the desert, slowly and firmly. I actually felt a deeper happiness and peace that the shifting feelings on the surface could not take away. This led to a sense of freedom in which even the trees seemed to "glow" with God's presence. It was as if God/Love was shining in and through all things. One evening, I wrote in my journal:

God is a luminous freedom! This freedom from self-attachment is a grace to be free in God. Freedom is everywhere in God/Love who is everywhere. His Love shines in us just as we are—in our hearts and in everything.

Dare I fly? Do I really have wings? Jesus is Lord shining everywhere humble, soft, gentle, and tender in glory.
This seems astounding since there is so much evil and
pain in this world. It is a paradox. Is it true? Going to
the window and looking out, I see again that it is true
everywhere. All the houses and trees and hills and sky
shine with Jesus's risen presence. It reminds me of Dio-
nysius the Areopagite's "Dazing Darkness."

My first reaction to this Easter insight was a strong feeling
I should not judge myself or others, but just accept myself and
everyone just as we are. But, it was a surprise that as I sensed the
luminosity, peace, and joy, a new struggle emerged. On the one
hand, I was attracted to the Light, while on the other hand, I was
also clinging to the Darkness. It seemed that the Darkness had
become familiar and even comfortable to me. And the Light was
something unknown. To tell the truth, I was a bit afraid.

I shared this paradox with Jim Conner. He said that certainly
there is love, light, and peace in the monastery. But in the world,
there is much pain, violence, fear, confusion, and even dread. So, a
contemplative today must expect to experience them often because
one does not enter the monastery to escape the world, but to
redeem it. The monastic takes all the pain of the world into the
monastery with him or her and then takes it to prayer. It becomes
his or her prayer for the redemption of the world. Jesus is being
crucified today in so many ways and in so many places. And the
forces that once crucified Him are at work in all of us. We cannot
turn away from pain and suffering into a mystical light. This does
not mean to cling to the suffering and deny joy. In our suffering,

God is exposing to us the forces we must deal with in our own ministry in the Church. These forces in us, in turn, expose how they are crucifying Jesus in the world around us.

Jim added that whom I call Jesus Forsaken is in modern humanity more than ever before in the history of the world. He needs us to minister to Him in this suffering of humanity and to help Him resurrect in people, bringing them into the Light. For this ministry, we need also to know the Light as I have now found. This is the task for the monastic too. But the identity of the monks with Jesus Crucified is of ultimate importance. This penance is grace for the other parts of the Mystical Body of Christ. In the pain and crosses that the monastics feel and embrace, they experience a real unity with Jesus Crucified.

On the other hand, Jesus is also risen and glorified. The Holy Spirit is the gift of His risen glory in each of us. But, His glory will not be complete until the Kingdom of Light and Life comes in all its fullness for all humankind. Therefore, the glory of Jesus not only gives the Cross its meaning, but our crosses as well. In our crosses, we go through the Cross into the light of Glory. Yet at the same time, we are part of humankind since this process of redemption is not yet finished for all humanity, including ourselves. So there will always be crosses in our lives.

As members of the Mystical Body of Christ, we will always express in our own bodies the tension of the Cross and the Glory, of death and resurrection, of Darkness and Light, as we make up what is still lacking, as Paul says, for the Kingdom's coming. So, when crosses come into our lives, we need to trust in God and remember that we are participating in His struggle to give birth to Himself in the hearts of all men and women—that they all may be one as Jesus prayed.

Growth in prayer, Jim said, is the growing ability to focus more and more on God and his initiatives and less and less on ourselves and the quality of our response. Yet, we will always

be forced to embrace the cross of our own self-knowledge and
the suffering of the human condition as such. The experience of
Darkness is to be held in dialectical tension with knowledge of the
Light and the Glory of God. Our faith is always that the Spirit of
God is in each person, including ourselves. Beyond the cross we
find in others; we must see God's Glory in order to help nurture
the Spirit that comes from that Glory in the lives of others. We
must accept the whole person by affirming his or her essential
goodness and addressing his or her existential pain he or she
is carrying. The Light of the Glory of God keeps us from being
pulled down by existential reality of our broken world. Remember that sometimes we can embrace our crosses with gratitude
and love—but not all the time or it would not be the Cross.

Jim also said that all humankind has been redeemed by Jesus.
We all are branches on the True Vine of life. The challenge is to
realize our spiritual condition and to learn from it in order to
bear fruit. We need to recognize Jesus and allow the Holy Spirit
to nurture our branch with new life that restores us to the like-
ness and image of God. This nurture and restoration is a process
of death and new life, of moving from Darkness into Light—it
is the Way of the Cross. God leaves us all free to accept or deny
Jesus's gift to us. This is the fundamental choice of our life as
Christians.

Jim concluded by saying that God cannot change our lives in
one experience of the Night. Someday, God may dig deeper and
deeper into your soul in another Dark Night until you grow into
your true self, who you ready really are, the way God created you.
Hearing these words, I had the impression that someday, I may
go through the second Night in order to discover my true self hidden from me by my past. It is the word God has spoken, creating
me through the Word. I thought of this later at a colloquium on
self-transformation. A priest of 40 years named Tony said that
he was wondering what of his self as a priest was really himself

and what was a "product" of his religious formation. I thought
to myself, *What of me is a product of my family and my life up
to now, and what is my real self that God created?*

One day on the BART, I noticed a woman with two small
pre-school children. She constantly yelled at them and spoke to
them about things way over their heads. At one point, she said,
"I wish you had not been born so I could get some peace!" I
could "feel" the pain going from the woman into her children.
I "saw" that this woman was distorting how God created these
children. She was making it more and more impossible for them
to see their true selves, their inherent goodness. And there was
another woman, who was very beautiful, sitting and reading a
book. Another child peeked over the back of her seat and asked
the woman a simple question. The woman ignored the child and
kept reading her book. Although she was beautiful to look at, she
was distorted inside. In both cases, I felt an almost unbearable
pain in my heart.

Another experience took place in Sausalito. Ann and I took
the day off to go to our favorite spot: Muir Woods. On the way
back, we stopped at Sausalito for lunch. Next to us was a table
with a number of "rich" and "beautiful" women with lots of
jewelry. They were drinking margaritas and discussing California topics. Suddenly, I felt cold. When we left the restaurant, we
passed a group of children with Down Syndrome. They were on
an outing and eating ice cream. The kids had dressed up for the
trip and had ice cream all over their faces and clothes. I felt an
inner love and joy for them. They were being their real selves, and
I sensed a special presence of Jesus with these kids.

Finally, one day I had lunch with my student friend named
Martha at the GTU. She told me that some years ago, she had an
operation on her back that ended up leaving her paralyzed from
the waist down. She was depressed for a good part of a year and
felt totally lost. Then, as she accepted her condition and embraced

it as her cross, she had a conversion. She began to feel that the cross made a sanctifying effect on her soul and that God was calling her to minister to the suffering of others. As she got better, she entered hospital ministry and then came to the GTU to take some classes. This made me think that my present cross may also be God calling me to a life of dialogue. But for now, I have to sit in my seat, as Dan said, until the bus arrives at its destination.

I had a final conversation with Jim about Merton's *The Inner Life*. He encouraged me to seek a spiritual community life that is contemplative, ecumenical, interfaith, gives service to the poor, and has as its goal the unity of the human family. As he talked, I thought to myself that what he described was like the Focolare. Jim again encouraged me to publish something about this Night journey I was undergoing and another one if it should happen. He said not to worry about pride. "People," he said, "constantly come to Gethsemani expressing the need for spiritual material that can help them as laypeople who are experiencing a Dark Night. We have nothing that is firsthand. And a spiritual story from a layperson is much better than a theoretical book." I promised I would; and now I that I am retired, I am fulfilling my promise.

When Easter arrived, I went with the Sisters of the Holy Family Convent to the famous Vigil Mass at the Oakland Cathedral. The liturgy began with 20 minutes of darkness during which "Decent into Hell" was played electronically. Then, the darkness began to lift a bit by a candlelight procession—a light in the darkness. You could see the light and yet feel the darkness around us. Then the Mass began. It had four parts, each related to the transvaluing of the four elements. First was fire that was transvalued as Christian Truth dispelling the darkness. Water was transvalued as Baptism in Christ wherein we rise to new life. Earth was transvalued as the Eucharist, the bread and wine that nourishes us in this new life. Air was transvalued as the Holy Spirit who brings us new life in union with God. The message was that God labors in and through all creation to make us new creatures, to make us His sons and daughters. I came away feeling a strong desire to be involved in this labor to transform humankind into one family of brothers and sisters.

CHAPTER 12

Family and Dialogue

I should add a few words about our life as a family. Our three children were in school. Kristy was going to Kindergarten—and Ann and I both cried as she got on the school bus for the first time. In the evenings, we had a good family life based on what we had all learned from the Focolare about living with Jesus in the midst. We were just like any other family with homework, dinner, and games, or taking a walk in the area of Walnut Creek where we lived. On weekends or holidays, we would take family trips. We enjoyed going to Fisherman's Wharf and Ghirardelli Square. We spent a lot of time in Golden Gate Park, especially walking down to the ocean. We discovered Angel Island and would take the boat out there and have lunch, climb the hill, and come home at dusk.

We were a tennis family, so would play tennis at the courts in Walnut Creek. We also liked to explore Tilden Park above Berkeley and ride on the merry-go-round. We would also go hiking in Mt. Diablo State Park near Walnut Creek. But I think our favorite short trip was over the Golden Gate Bridge and up to Muir

Woods with all the redwood trees with a stop at dusk at Sausalito.
A few times, we would drive down to Monterey and get on the
17-mile drive along the coast that is beautiful! We would stop
along the way until we got to Carmel. Sometimes we visited the
Carmel Mission where Fr. Serra is buried. Otherwise we would
go to the beach and to the town.

In other words, we were an ordinary family enjoying ourselves
in a beautiful part of the world. While inside, I was struggling, I
seemed to be able to function well at the GTU and at home. The
children were too young to really notice any difference in me. I
asked them later in life, and the only thing that the older boys
noticed was that at times, I would retreat to the bedroom to be
alone. Dan came to dinner a number of times. We went to a local
parish, and Ann and I even went on a Marriage Encounter. At
the parish, we met other families and did things with them that
were fun.

As I said, a true Dark Night begins and ends with a specific
moment that you always remember. For me, it ended when I was
driving from San Francisco to Lafayette and stopped at a gas
station. As I pumped the gas, I felt and saw something "fly" out
of me into the sky. From that moment, the Darkness was gone.

The transformation in the Dark Night and the experience
with the Jesuits, Franciscans, and the Dominicans produced a
deep sensitivity to many aspects of the spiritual life. This new
experience and my studies opened my mind to deeper compar-
isons with Buddhism. As I entered the Buddhist-Christian dialogue, I found myself able to connect to Buddhist scholars and
monastics in a deeper way. Once at a dialogue, Hans Kung was
responding to the famous Buddhist scholar Masao Abe. He did
not fully understand what Abe was saying, so I stepped in and
helped explain. Later, Hans asked me to have lunch with him. In
our conversation, he found out to his surprise that I was a Catholic. He said, "You seem more like a Buddhist and at home with

the Buddhists." I said that I find that I now have a deeper unity with Buddhists due to my growth in Catholic spirituality. Later, he and I would become good friends in a dialogue group formed by Masao Abe and John Cobb called the Abe-Cobb Group. As my work in the dialogue in the United States and Asia developed, in 1986, Cardinal Arinze, then President of what is now the Pontifical Council for Interreligious Dialogue (PCID), asked me to be their consultor for Buddhism. I have helped organize the PCID dialogues with Buddhism to this day.

CHAPTER 13

Omen of a Second Dark Night

On September 4, 1991, I found myself feeling mentally, physically, and emotionally distressed. At first, I thought I was becoming depressed and anxious. But after a while, I began to wonder if it might be the beginning of a second Dark Night. It had been 12 years since the first one. Since I could not find a spiritual director where I lived, I turned to the writings of John of the Cross about what he termed "the dark night of the spirit."

At the beginning of John's writings, he gave a description of what one is like after the first Night: "In the new state, as one liberated from a cramped prison cell, it goes about the things of God with much more freedom and satisfaction of spirit and with more abundant interior delight than it did in the beginning before entering the night of sense." (2N 1.1)

That was true for me. I had developed my work and publications in the Buddhist-Christian dialogue both in Asia and the United States. In 1986, I was invited by Cardinal Arinze to be a consultant for the Pontifical Council for Interreligious Dialogue for which he was President. This led to my participation in a number of Vatican sponsored dialogues.

Then, John went on to say that before a second Night, a person may experience inner "disturbances" and "conflicts" that are "like omens or messengers of the coming night of the spirit." (2N 1.1) He said that this is because the person still possesses "habitual imperfections." John notes that this is due to their "old self," or the condition of the self that is not as God created it. This false self needs to be "purged" so the "new self" may emerge, that is, one's true self is discovered and lived. John writes that God wishes "to strip them in fact of this old self and clothe them with the new, which was created according to God." (2N 3.3)

I certainly had habitual imperfections, and I came to experience a particular "omen" shortly after my father died. I traveled by myself to San Diego to visit my mother. We would sit up and talk into the night. One night as I lay in bed, I suddenly felt overwhelmingly terrified! But, in some way, it seemed strangely familiar. As I lay there, I began to remember feeling that way as a child and a youth. There was a deep fear of being there in the house but also a sense I could not survive anywhere else. At the same time, I feared that my father would come through the door angry at me. I got out of bed and went back to my mother who was in the den at the desk. I sat on the couch and started talking to her about this "inner disturbance." She nodded knowingly, which surprised me.

She said quietly: "You know I was young and did not understand how Jim's behavior was affecting you. But over the years, I came to realize how frightened you were of everything. When we had Barbara (my sister), I told Jim that he could not treat her like he treated you. I would not stand for it. He did not answer me. But he did treat her different. Even then, Barbara called him 'the tyrant.' Remember that during the War, Jim had polio. We lived in Ocean Beach just right across the street from the beach. One day, you got out of the gate and went down the street pulling a toy duck on a string. When we found that you were missing, we ran down the street looking for you. Jim had to stop and rest because of the effects of the polio on his legs. We finally got to a corner where there was a gas station, and there you were standing with your toy duck. Jim got very upset with you for the first time. He seemed to realize that with his disability, he could not keep you safe. Once, we took you to Disneyland when it first opened. In the parking lot, you saw the train that goes around the park. You started jumping up and down with excitement, and said that you wanted to go on the train. Jim picked you up and shook you violently. He told you that you could be hurt and needed to say right by him so he could keep you safe. I felt like Jim shook the life out of you."

When I returned home, I realized that the fear I felt at Mom's house had been repressed deep inside me and that it would come at times in a mixture of fear, anxiety, and depression. I told Ann about what happened in San Diego and that I felt I needed guidance. At the beginning of the first Night, Dan had asked me if I wanted spiritual direction or psychological support. Since I did not know of any spiritual directors, I told Ann that I wanted a therapist to help guide me with what was surfacing. It turned out that a new psychiatrist came to town from Chicago because her husband had taken a job at Purdue. Her name was Karen. I called a therapist friend in Chicago to ask about Karen's reputation. My friend actually knew her and said that she had a good reputation for working well with people. So, I began going to her. It soon became clear to both of us that a deep inner process had begun.

At this point, I had John of the Cross to read in order to understand what I was going through and what it meant. And, I had Karen to help me psychologically. But, I would soon discover that God gave me the most important support and guidance in the constant presence of Jesus Forsaken and Mary. They had become close to me since I began practicing the spirituality of the Focolare. Now, they became my spiritual companions during the second Night. They would often be with me in ways that helped me through the Darkness.

As it turned out, this Night would last for years—eight years, to be precise. While I have a dozen notebooks filled with entries about what took place, most of what I wrote is too personal for me to share. So, I have chosen to share just a few important events that also indicate the overall process of my Dark Night.

CHAPTER 14

A Child Appears

At the beginning of this eruption, I felt depressed and began to have memories of how insecure I had been with feeling I was unwanted and unworthy all mixed together that defined myself. I would often sit in prayer by myself and reflect on what was happening inside me. Once, I closed my eyes and found myself standing still in the middle of a dirt road. Ahead of me, a child of about four or five was crawling out of a ditch on the left side of the road and was walking to the middle of the road. He stood there anxious, moving his body around but with his feet fixed. He looked back to the side of the road and then at me. He was covered with mud and did not have any clothes on. I had no idea of what this was all about ... so I shared it with Karen. She talked about what she called an "inner child." She said the inner child reflects who we were as a child and still defines our self in the present.

Later, I experienced Jesus introducing me to the child in the road. It was like the two of us were with Jesus behind us with His arms around our shoulders. My impression was that Jesus was entrusting the child to my care. I asked Him, "But aren't you going to care for this child in me?" Jesus answered, "I will care for him through you. I have made you the person you really are, and now you must take care of this child in you that you have come to recognize." The next day, I awoke with the sense that I was alone with this child and had to care for him myself. And at the same time, my own self was somehow still this child. This was really hard to understand.

The next afternoon, I took a long walk in the park. At the end of the walk, I sat down and brought to mind the child. I told him that Dad did love him but just did not show it. It was a tragic mistake. Now, I will love him ... will love my self ... and so will Jesus. I said that he and I have to believe that with God's grace, he will be healed. Later, it occurred to me that I was the one who will be healed. It seemed that I was being introduced to a source of my false self ... the dirt-covered child that I have carried in me all my life. God wants me to discover my true self that has always been in the heart and mind of God.

Another day at Mass, I felt like I was not able to move—like I cannot do anything myself to deal with what I was experiencing. In prayer I said, "What can I do?" Turning to the first reading of that day, I found Is. 35: 4–7: "Say to those whose hearts are frightened: Be strong, fear not! Here is your God, he comes with vindication." The song we had sung at Mass was "Be not afraid, I am with you. I have called you each by name. Come and follow me. I will bring you home, I love you and you are mine." I understood that there is nothing I could do but let God do what He wants to do. I just need to have faith.

At one point, I thought that what seemed to be happening to me involved a constant eruption of memories and emotions from beyond my control. I remembered Dan telling me one of the rules of discernment: that if the experience was unexpected, a surprise that does not feel like just a result of my own train of thought, then it was due to the work of God in my soul. I remembered that Dan also said that God will finish what He has begun.

One day after Mass, I was moved to listen to the voice of Jesus: "Love me in others. That is the way that the loving and kind part of yourself, your real self in the image of God, will grow in positive ways." Another day, a kind of image came to my mind: The child, myself and Jesus sitting, with Jesus holding us both together. I asked Jesus to heal the child, but he said, "No. You have to heal him." "How?" I responded. "By giving him what you gave your own children." Again, I asked, "How?" "Cherish yourself like you do your own children. Soothe yourself with the love you have given them."

One day, I met a Hindu friend who was a professor in engineering. He was very devout and led the Hindu community in our city. He asked me how I was doing. I told him just a bit about what I was going though. He said, "If you repress your karma, it saps your strength and causes physical and psychological illness. We must let it up from the soul and look at it, experience the pain, and let it go. It helps to call on God's healing spirit to heal the karmic wound. But we also must ask for the spirit of forgiveness. If we hold to the pain and remember, 'He did this to me!' the karmic effect increases. So, we must forgive and let it go into God's mercy." I was surprised that he seemed to understand what I was going through from his experience in Hinduism. It made me think that this process is universal. God has ways of working in the lives of all people on earth. And over the months, when I would remember particular events that formed my false self, I would look at it, feel the pain, accept it, and then care for myself by letting it go. Once, God seemed to say "Yes. Care for yourself as I am caring for you."

CHAPTER 15

Emotions and Forgiveness

As time passed, I no longer experienced the child. Rather, pain, grief, despair, and anger became stronger as more memories were brought to light. One day after Mass, sitting in the chapel in prayer, the words of the Gospel reading of that day, "Let the little children come unto me" came from inside me. They were followed by Jesus's words: "I will take him into My heart. I will take your wounds into My heart of love. Don't cling to the child— this part of you that has to be seen to be healed is now put into my heart. I will heal the child in you. Now, care for yourself and love Me in others as I love in you. You are not finished yet, but you are well along. Be at peace."

As it turned out, peace took some time. For example, due to the memories that kept coming up, the strongest emotion I felt was anger. I often felt extremely upset and angry at everything and everyone. One evening, I drove out to the Tippecanoe Battle-field Park and walked among the graves. As I walked across the bridge over the creek where the Native Americans attacked the American soldiers, I felt exhausted and devastated by memories.

This made me angrier at everything and everyone. I was angry about my lifetime warped by what happened with Dad. And, I realized that I had repressed that anger throughout my life, and that made me angry too. Another emotion was grief. My grief over how I had been affected over the years was profoundly upsetting. I realized that I keep a distance between myself and others by an inner wall to protect myself. I asked God about this and He said, "When you harden your heart, you cannot hear My voice. Soften your heart with your tears and listen for My voice." The tears came on my birthday when I received a card from my mother. She wrote, "I hope this year will bring you a lot of peace and you will be able to receive the love so many people feel for you and that the rest of your life will be productive and satisfying and happy with a lot of love which you deserve." As I read those few words, I cried and felt the inner wall come down.

One day, I understood in prayer that the place inside where I am grieving deep in my soul is the same place where God is now loving and healing me. Also, in this dark and painful place in my heart, I was experiencing more and more a relation with Jesus Forsaken. On the Cross, He became one with all who suffer. It is He that opens my wounds and shows me the damage. It is like a hidden love washing over the pain. Tears of grief mixed with tears of love. This enables me to accept with more peace what God is showing me about myself. So too, Jesus Forsaken within my heart is asking me to not focus on Him and His work in me, but to turn to loving others. Even if I *feel* no love to give, I am always free to *choose* to love.

Once in prayer, Jesus Forsaken appeared. I looked more closely and saw that hHe was risen. When I saw this, I began to panic. I cried and said, "But now you will be what I am not." Jesus said, "You are afraid not to be broken." I thought, *He is right. But, I don't know what to do about it. It is who I have always been.* The next day, I wrote, "I feel called to be well and yet it goes against my identity ... my self as it is. But I maintain this identity by my will for a reason. What is that reason? I just can't let it go; it makes me afraid. It seems like I am trying to be well and at the same time trying not to be well. It is an inner struggle that I have only now realized. Right now the conflict is intense."

Advent began and I was moved by reading Isaiah 9:1–7:

The people that walked in darkness have seen a great light; on those who live in a land of deep shadow a light has shone.... For the yoke that was weighing on him, the bar across his shoulders, the rod of his oppressor, these you break as on the day of Midian.... For there is a child born for us, a son given to us, and dominion is laid on his shoulders; and this is the name they give him: Wonder Counselor, Mighty God, Eternal Father, Prince of Peace.

In prayer: "I healed you in the past. Now this process is the love of God for you. Don't worry. Believe in My love for you even if you don't feel it ... you will feel it later."

At a certain point, I realized after going to confession that I needed to forgive. I had to forgive my father and myself. How? In prayer, I saw a child giving me a flower. I took it. It seems like forgiveness is like that. It is a gift that we give or accept. God seemed to be asking me to take the flower of forgiveness, into my heart. Turing to Jesus, I prayed for the gift of forgiveness and He put his arms around my shoulder. As He did, another flower bloomed in my soul. I thought that this is like a row of forgiveness switches. You turn them on one at a time. God seems to be asking me to turn one on each day, to accept His forgiveness of me each day, to forgive myself each day, to forgive my father each day. In doing so, it is like I am receiving a brick to build a new house ... a house of acceptance in God where I can live my true self in God's love.

Doing what God is asking me was not easy, and for weeks I struggled with the wounds within me. I could say, "I forgive those who have wounded me and I forgive the self-inflicted wounds." But these seemed to be just words. I felt that I could not heal this situation. It is like the camel that needs to be unburdened. The camel cannot take off the burdens himself. I asked God for the grace to let him work in me. That evening at a Focolare meeting, I felt something change in me. I felt a new sense of trust . . . of entrustment to God's forgiving love. The next day at Mass, it seemed like Jesus danced. This was a surprise! I wrote about a prayer experience I had that day:

> Jesus was pouring seeds of flowers of love from His mouth—His words are love—into my heart where they take root and grow. Jesus puts His arms around me— encouraging me. He puts His hands on my head—blessing me with His spirit of forgiveness. To receive this spirit of God is to receive the power to love myself, God, and others. Here is a power not of dominance over me like with my father, but an empowering of me to love God, myself, and others. To be honest, I am still weak and resist this gift given my old self. But God is stronger! Trust that Jesus will win the fight. In the end, He just says: "Be at peace, care for yourself, and love Me in others."

Later, I picked up a flower holder that belonged to my mother. Looking at it, I thought, *I wish my childhood had been a happy one.* As I completed this thought, Jesus Forsaken said to me, "Then you would have never met Me."

CHAPTER 16

The Second Dark Night

As this healing of memories came to an end, the second Dark Night for the purification and transformation of one's soul began. And, I realized that I needed to turn to John of the Cross for guidance. John introduces the dark night of the spirt in the following way: "This dark night is an inflow of God into the soul, which purges it of his habitual ignorance and imperfections, natural and spiritual, and which contemplatives call infused contemplation or mystical theology." (2N 5.1) He says that this causes two things. First is that the inflow of divine Light is so strong that it blinds the soul. The person experiences this as Darkness. Second, this Light exposes the impurities, which causes the person to experience pain, affliction, torment, weakness, miseries, and wretchedness. Given this state, persons suffer so much that they "undergo such agony and pain that the soul would consider death a relief." (2N 5.6) John notes that this Night strips the person "of habitual affections and properties of the old self to which the soul is strongly united, attached, and conformed ... that the soul at the sight of its miseries feels that it is melting away and being undone by a cruel spiritual death." (2N 6.1)

Finally, John uses the metaphor of a "fire consuming the tarnish and rust of metal," quoting Ezekiel 24:11: "Place it also thus empty on the embers that its metal may become hot and melt and its unclearness be taken away from it and its rust consumed." I would add that what is removed are the elements of the old self that are created by choices and experiences in this world so that the true self can be found and lived in the Light and Love of God. This, according to John, prepares the soul for union with God.

Well ... this description did not make me very happy. However, after the prelude presented above, I lived at peace for some time. But then came what I can only characterize as a decent into hell. It began on a Friday afternoon. I began to tremble all over my body, and tears flowed down my face. The condition seemed to affect my soul, and not just my emotions and thoughts. There was a tangible Darkness that reached the core of my being and encompassed the world. I was plunged into this Darkness feeling only fear, doubt, despair, and hopelessness. Suddenly, it seemed I was dying. The Darkness in my mind and my heart was hard as a rock.

I drove to Horticulture Park where I took a walk every day. I just walked and cried all afternoon until it was dark. In the midst of my painful walk in the park one day, I experienced Jesus taking my face and turning it toward His face. He said, "Jesus Forsaken is all. There is nothing but Him in your pain." My thoughts following this experience in the park are expressed in the note I wrote when I got home:

Because of my shame for what I see now in myself, I

cannot stand people saying good things about me. So,

I say bad things to myself and others to fit how I think

of myself and push people away. I only see the negative in myself and the world. What can I do? Nothing. I can only look at Jesus Forsaken—the painful love of God for me as I now see myself. Seeing this, it seems that I have lived a lie all my life. This lie seems like a cold brick wall. I made myself this way—this wall. Now I am forced to look at it and feel the self-inflicted pain, and the pain I have brought to others. I am also facing Jesus Forsaken at the same time. Facing Jesus, the Truth, I face the truth about the wall that is myself, my false self. I am the wall that separates me from the Kingdom of God, from the joy of the saved. I am facing the lie that I have made as a wall. Jesus descended into hell. Now he descends into my hell, the hell of who I am. This is not what the Word/Jesus created for me, but what I have created for myself.

The next day, I felt self-hatred all day long . . . just pure self-loathing. At the end of the day, I was in tears because of the intensity of the feelings. I can say that I wanted to reject this lie, but that was a thought. The feelings in me ran deeper than thoughts about myself. I believe the lie was at a deep level in my soul, and then I felt I was being punished since that was what I felt that I deserved. In prayer:

Accept yourself with this deep wound. It is your cross and it will not be too much for you. See My Face in this cross, and find My Face in others who are suffering. Love Me in others, and let others love you. In this mutual love, you will find Me in your midst. Turn pain into love, and in this way, you will be connected to others more deeply. Your spirituality is communal, so go to God through others.

The next day, the feeling was fear. It stemmed from a dream. I was a boy at table, eating with others. We ran out of macaroni, and I offered to get some more. I stood up proud and put on a suit and tie to go to the store. But the store was out of macaroni. I had to return home without the macaroni, and I felt I let the others down. I felt ashamed. That feeling of self-hatred connected to shame made me afraid when I woke up. I felt that was not adequate to get things done. I was a failure. So, I was afraid that I would not make it since I was so inadequate. That is what I believed and felt deep inside. Only death awaited me.

CHAPTER 17

Epiphany

One night, something "touched" me. I woke up, and there seemed an inner pressure that was really strong pulling me down and down. I seemed to go down deep inside myself. This pressure made me afraid. I prayed to Jesus, and to my great surprise, I found Mary holding my face. She said, "I too had to be strong and affirm myself, especially after Joseph died. It was not easy being a widow in those days."

I responded, "But I am afraid."

"Many people who listened to Jesus were afraid too. Some rejected Him out of that fear."

"Were you afraid?"

"Yes. Remember when the angel came? That made me afraid. It was unexpected, a surprise. But I said 'Yes.' Now Jesus is asking for your 'yes.' That is why I am here now. You must say your yes like I did at the foot of the Cross. He wants to free you from what is impure here deep inside you that you now feel, but He never forces anyone. So, don't be afraid ... don't let your fear stop you. Say your yes to Him too."

Mary seemed to back up, and I found myself wrestling within myself: "I am afraid. Who will care for me?" "Jesus will be there always." "I can't make it." "Jesus will be the basis of your life." "I will get in trouble." "No. You did before you had Jesus ... now it is different." "But I have to kill my father!" "Not your real father, but the lie he lived. You have to let him go and give all of yourself to Jesus."

I saw myself seated again in front of Jesus. He stood up and looked at me. I said, "Yes" and got up. We hugged each other.

Mary said, "Jesus continued to care for me after His death both directly or through John. He will always care for you directly or through Ann and others too."

Later while walking in the park: "Jesus is the savior of your life. So, your life is good. Don't be afraid to live your life; it is good."

At Mass that evening, in Darkness, I thought about John's Prologue—all life comes through Jesus. My real life came and comes through the Word/Jesus, and I can accept it or reject it. I am terrified that I cannot live the life he gave me, my true self—I will go crazy. "Don't be afraid to accept the life that Jesus created for you. He will help you live it, and you CAN live it. It is God's gift of love for you!" The next day, I struggled with my feelings about my father at church. Mary said, "You can carry the good memories of your father. Remember how he smiled at you before he died. That was your real father." This happened on the Feast of Mary Mother of God. It was gray outside, but a ray of light came through the window of the church. I felt peace and happiness for the first time. When I looked in my mind, I found Jesus and Mary both. I had the sense that they are never alone. There are many others with them, and they seemed all to be doing something. "Keep your eyes only on Jesus." At Mass, it seemed that I saw Him in everyone. All the faces seemed like His face.

In light of these experiences, I reflected on myself. Now, I see that God made me in a certain way, and that He allowed things to happen to me that formed me as I am. Myself and all persons are in some ways disabled by their life experience. Any person who has a "disability" is especially loved by God. Jesus is one with us all as we are . . . this is the Good News. God is simple: Abba, Daddy. Maybe now God wants to heal my disabilities in some way.

Some days later, I returned into the Darkness. At the Focolare, I felt in this Darkness drawn to look closely at a picture of Jesus Forsaken. I wrote;

I saw Jesus with new eyes. He seemed so human and so warm. I felt love for Him and a desire to hug Him. Later, when I remembered this picture, I was moved to tears and felt the desire to love and embrace Him ... something new for me. He is silent, but I felt the words "Just love Me wherever you find Me." And it seemed that I found him everywhere. He died on the Cross and became one with all who suffer. I felt the words, "Yes, embrace and love Me in yourself and in everyone else you meet." I felt overwhelmed by His immense suffering in all people. I felt the words, "Don't worry. The world is in My hands, not yours. I am taking care of every-thing. All you have to do is love Me in yourself and oth-ers you meet. That is all." Then, these word followed: "Let me be God. Just love me in yourself and others. That is all." I cried.

I remembered the passage in Second Corinthians:

> We are only the earthen vessels that hold a treasure ... We
> are in difficulties on all sides, but never cornered; we see
> no answer to our problems, but never despair; we have
> been persecuted, but never deserted; knocked down, but
> never killed; always, wherever we may be, we carry with
> us in our body the death of Jesus, so that the life of Jesus,
> too, may always be seen in our body. Indeed, while we
> are still alive, we are consigned to our death every day,
> for the sake of Jesus, so that in our mortal flesh the life
> of Jesus, too, may be openly shown. So, death is at work
> in us, but life in you. (2 Cor. 4: 7–12)

CHAPTER 18

Darkness and Light

The darkness was a painful place of "dryness, conflicts, and emptiness," as John says. (2N 9.2) It seemed like the pain comes from two lives that are battling within me. Which is the truth? On the one hand is my life as it has been, and on the other is a life that seems to be emerging from the Darkness. At times, the former seems to be my real life, and what is emerging seems a lie. At other times, it was the opposite. In both times, it is a constant painful struggle. I feel that this is a very strange conflict. But, John said that at times, "Everything seems so very strange even though a person is the same as always." (2N 9.5)

When I was in pain, I wept, but I was not overwhelmed because I embraced Jesus Forsaken—who is the peak of love poured out on the poor, the sinner, the person who suffers. As pain pierced my heart, I thought about Jesus Forsaken. He took all the suffering in the world into His heart on the Cross. Finding Him in the darkness reminded me that I am sharing in God's Son's sacrifice for the good of humankind. It includes suffering with God in myself and others out of love. But this was hard to believe ... to understand. On the other hand, I sensed that I was different! I am not the way I used to be. I thought, *What I am now, I don't know. Who I am now, I don't know. What my relationship with God is, I don't know. It is hidden in the Darkness.*

After a number of months, the painful Darkness that had surrounded me changed a bit to a more peaceful Darkness that seemed to be full of God. The emptiness of God in Darkness now seemed to be, in fact, a fullness of God in Darkness. The Darkness has a kind of divine texture that seemed like a luminosity in the Darkness. This texture of Light seemed to provide an impulse to love others. In personal terms, I could find and speak in prayer to Jesus Forsaken in the Darkness who leads me to love from His presence within me. I now experience this Light coming down from heaven on each person, illuminating their beauty in God's love for them. This ray of Light is like a path that leads to deeper union with God. My experience has been of rays of Light coming down on each thing in creation, not just persons. To see each being, animate and inanimate, as containing a ray of Light that is God's love makes them, indeed, all creation, seem so different—lovable! It is a Light in the Darkness that displays the preciousness of all things.

John notes that "sometimes the contemplation shines less forcibly so they may have the opportunity to observe and even rejoice over the work being achieved, for then these good effects are revealed ... So too, when the flame stops acting upon the wood, there is a chance to see how much the wood has been enkindled by it." (2N 10.6)

The experience of this lighter Darkness eventually passed. Once while in prayer, God said, "You joined Jesus when you converted and you journeyed together into the Church. He took you into the Focolare where you journeyed into My will—My love—for you. Now, Jesus has stopped and pointed at your crippled legs. You have looked down and seen that you were crippled."

Then, I looked up, and God was gone. I felt that everyone was gone. I was alone with my crippled legs waiting to be healed in a Dark Night. Later at Mass, I felt in a thicker Darkness: alone, sick, afraid, sad, and lost. But I said, "Yes." At the same time, I understood that this "Yes" is something to be lived with Ann and my children, with God in the church, with Mary in her work—the Focolare—and in my own work for the Pontifical Council for Interreligious Dialogue with Buddhism.

A few days later, Ann and I were visiting friends in the country and walking down a dirt road past cornfields. Some of the fields had been harvested, leaving only stubble. I thought, *This is how I feel.* This Darkness had been going on for many terrible years, and I felt reduced to stubble. I wanted to say, "Why?" like Jesus Forsaken said on the Cross. Then the tears came up.

As the days and weeks passed, it seemed that I was constantly angry over everything. Masao Abe, the great Japanese Buddhist scholar, was at Purdue working with me. He noticed my angry mood. He told me that in Buddhism, below anger is pain. The anger needs to be faced, understood, and mindfully accepted until the pain reveals itself. Masao also said that my anger is a No, and there is a Yes below it. Reflecting on what Masao said, I began accepting the painfulness Darkness within me. By grace, I was able to say "Yes" to God below my pain.

A few days later, I was walking in Horticulture Park and stopped at the grove of huge evergreen trees. I called it the "Grove of Tears" since over the years, I would go there to cry. I stood in the grove and suddenly thought of my dad. It was painful, and I felt my heart break. I had to hold a tree limb to stabilize myself. It felt like I would break in two. Suddenly, I called out, "Dad!" In my mind, he approached me and we embraced. He was in his later years. I had to stop the image since I could not stand the huge wave of emotion. It seemed like the emotional chains that had enslaved me for my life dropped off. I felt free from this slavery to what my father did to me. I saw him as a man living his own anger that covered his own inner pain.

A week later, I was taking a walk at night alone, feeling very weak. It was October and there was a beautiful harvest moon. Walking up the street with large trees on each side, it seemed like each one was standing by itself—large and strong. It reminded me of the time I walked at night through a dark Zen monastic complex in Kyoto with each of the buildings seeming to be large and strong like these trees. "Where does this strong life come from? Why do I see it so clearly in the moonlight?" Then I prayed to God to help me understand this. I felt like my prayer became like a prayer of quiet. But it was different in that I could move around and feel natural, and my faculties were not overwhelmed.

I thought to myself that perhaps the phases of the moon are like this dark journey to discover one's whole true self. As the moon becomes more and more whole in the darkness, it reflects the light of the sun more and more. Eventually it becomes a "full moon," fully itself with all its surface ridges and valleys. One becomes one's true self by participating in God, and reflecting the light of God. When the moon is fully itself, it shines with the light of the sun on the trees, revealing what they truly are. So, in the transforming union with God, a person does not "look" at himself or herself but at others with the love of God shining on them, helping to reveal who they truly are in the mind of God. God is Love ... so the Light of God is Love. To reflect that Light is to be love for others. Transforming union leads to being fully love for others so that one can see them as God who is Love sees them. The moon does not reflect the light of the sun to itself, but to the trees, illuminating them for what they are.

At that point, I looked at the craters on the moon. The light of the sun does not remove those craters, but they too reflect the light. It is the same with our imperfections. They remain as part of who we are. Even our wounds—the ones I have been seeing lately—when they are healed leave scars that reflect the love of God.

The moon is empty of itself and in its silence reflects the light of the sun like a mirror. But in being empty of itself, in that reflection, in that moonlight, it is fully giving itself. So, when we are empty of ourselves, we can reflect the Light of God that is Love. We can be fully ourselves as gifts for the others. This is what the trees are for me as I walk by them in the moonlight. I felt a deep unity with each tree ... like every tree was in my heart and I was in its being.

So, now I see that like the moon, I do not have to do anything. I just need to let God be God and let God lead me to that place where God becomes more and more, as the moon follows its path to become full. I thought that union with God was union between two persons (God and a human being). But now I see it as growing into the Life of God, the Light of God, the Love of God that reveals who I am—fully my true self. I do talk with God and He may do something, but at a deeper level, it is what Paul says: it is no longer he that lives but Christ within him who lives.

CHAPTER 19

Thanksgiving Time

By Thanksgiving, I began to see both myself and other people differently. As John says, "The soul never remains in one state, but everything is ascent or descent." (2N 18.3) It was like I began quietly rediscovering myself in a deeper mutual relationality that includes God, humanity, and nature. I seemed to feel a new process of reconnecting in a different way with people, God, Jesus, Mary, and nature. It did not happen all at once, but slowly.

For example, Jesus Forsaken no longer came and went but was always there. He never moved or disappeared in the Darkness. Once, I experienced being taken by Jesus Forsaken off the Cross to where He was risen. The darkness shined with light in which Christ was King caring for His people, protecting them, and washing their feet. Mary was with Him, and she was given to me by her Son as my mother. I also remember thinking of when Paul said, "It is no longer me who lives but Christ within me who lives." I sensed my true self as a word of Word/Jesus residing in me.

One other thing in this regard. I visited the Focolare in Chicago, and they had a book out on the prayers of St. Teresa of

Avila. I had read her *Interior Castle* and her *Life* at the Jesuit School of Theology. One prayer that caught my eye was made after she re-discovered the humanity of Jesus as crucified and risen being her friend before His ascension. This is like what I have experienced since He pulled me down from the Cross. In prayer, we were together, but I could not touch or embrace Him. It reminded me of when He told Mary Magdalene not to touch Him.

There is another aspect to this prayerful relationship. Before, He was either away from me some distance or before me close by. Now, I experience Him within me. And when I look at someone, it is He looking at that person through my eyes. But this was not something permanent. I vacillated between being with Christ within me, and being just myself. When it was the former, I felt myself, whole, full, connected, and loving. Then, I seemed to lose Him and fall back into the Darkness.

I talked to Masao Abe about this a few days later. Abe asked me if Christ is always there even if I am not aware of Him, or if actually Christ comes and goes. I told him that while He seems to come and go, I know Christ is always there. Abe said, "If that is the case, the advice in Buddhism is to entrust yourself fully to this new reality with humility. The inner Reality, your true self, what we call your Buddha-nature, is slowly realizing itself in what you experience."

As I thought about this the next morning, I sensed that in both religions there is an act of faith, an act of letting go, or entrusting, of allowing. I am still afraid of doing this entirely. Then, as I watched the sun coming up, I allowed myself to let go. As the Darkness lifted, I felt a surge of life welling up within like an inner fountain. I said to myself, "This is morning!"

In that morning, I sensed an infinite Circle that is God. I was at the center of the Circle. And all other things in the world were at the Center as well. Later, I looked at my shoe beside the bed. I sensed that it was there for me as a gift from God. Everything in the whole Circle is interrelated and has brought about this shoe as a gift. All is gift. I felt full of gratitude. All things are themselves gifts for me from all in the infinite Circle of God. Everything in the world is like my shoe. Everything is a gift from God's infinite Love. We need to cherish everyone and every being we encounter as gifts.

Later, I found myself descending into the Night. As I did, Jesus seemed to be asking me to let Mary help me. As I descended into the Darkness, I looked into myself. But then it seemed that Mary had me look outside myself. I was in Chicago and noticed a boy with Down Syndrome. I also saw a kid riding in his dad's broken down truck. It struck me that the Light does not destroy the darkness of the world. We are all broken in some way. I cannot run away from it ... I am always in *samsara*—suffering in different ways. Mary as a mother especially loves all her broken children. She sees us as made of gold even if that gold is hidden in a dirty rag, as the Buddhists say. As our mother, she loves us as we are in our brokenness. Mary wants to care for me with Jesus Forsaken ... and wants me to love her Son in each person I meet.

A week later, I went to Luminosa—the Focolare's retreat center in Hyde Park, New York—for our winter retreat. Shortly after I arrived, I came down with the flu. I was stuck in my room but felt the presence of Mary caring for me. I wanted to be with the others. But then I discovered in the illness the presence of Jesus Forsaken. Mary showed Him to me as her Son who was one with me in my sickness. When I felt better, I went to the meetings. Once while listening to a talk, I felt one with the others. The true self I was discovering came to light in the unity with everyone. I felt a sense of peaceful belonging. I felt connected to people with all my flaws. Mary and Jesus were there too.

CHAPTER 20

God, Jesus, the Holy Spirit, and Mary

As time went on in the Darkness, I felt more and more strongly at different times that Jesus would visit me. Then, I understood that they are not only one in me but also with me. John writes, "His Majesty frequently gives it joy by paying it visits of spiritual delight. For the immense love that Christ, the Word, has cannot long endure the sufferings of his beloved without responding." (2N 19.4)

These visits seemed wonderful, but I was still in Darkness. Then at Mass, I sensed Jesus asking to be my servant. I felt surprised and had the sense that this was not right. Then, I remembered Jesus washing the disciples' feet. Only if He is with me can He serve me. But then I read in John that "These souls obtain from God what, with pleasure, they ask of Him. David accordingly declares, "Delight in God and he will grant you the petitions of your heart [Ps. 37.4]." (2N 20.2) Both of these visits, according to John, indicate that one is coming to the end of the Dark Night of the Spirit.

After these visits, in my mind I saw a boy in a box in front of me. He was upset and hiding from the world. I looked at him with pity. Then, Jesus was sitting with me looking at him with love. I cried and put my head on Jesus's shoulder. This image occurred a second time. Only then did I realize that the new understanding of my own distorted experience of myself could help me see with tears the distortions of others like this boy in his box. And with Jesus with me, I can be His hands reaching out and caring for others in their boxes. I felt that God was asking me to do this.

The next morning, I had a new sense of the Holy Spirit being with me too. It seemed that this whole Night is the work of the Holy Spirit—the Light or Fire causing the Darkness or the luminosity filling in the Darkness. I realized with the Holy Spirit was the "atmosphere" of this trial. With Him, I experience breathing in this atmosphere with each breath that surrounds me like an invisible air. It is an atmosphere of Love unseen in the Darkness. I also saw that the Holy Spirit is the atmosphere of Love that I can one day breathe with others in Paradise. I would later read from John's Spiritual Canticle about "the breath of spiration of the Holy Spirit from God to her [the soul] and from her to God." (CB 39.2)

On another morning, I remembered what Enzo Fondi, Director of the Center for Interreligious Dialogue at the Focolare Center in Italy, once said to me about the journey I am on. He said that since I was a member of the Work of Mary, Mary would have a hand in leading me on this journey, holding me by the hand. So, I felt the desire to consecrate myself again to Mary. I did so. Then, I prayed to the Holy Spirit that He would eventually bring me into a deeper participation in the Work of Mary.

Some hours later, I had the sense that I was not alone in the Darkness. I felt the deep atmosphere of the Holy Spirit spirating unity in which I felt the presence of all of the Work of Mary. Mary covered us with her mantle, and under it there was God who seemed like an infinite golden globe of Light. Mary brought me to the globe, and it seemed to somehow enter me while still remaining with me. Then, I heard, "We accept you." By "we," I thought of the Trinity and I replied, "How can you accept me like this? I cannot even accept myself." Mary replied, "Only you do not accept yourself. All are lovable children of God. No matter what their condition, they are accepted and loved by God. Love yourself. You are a child of God."

Later, I felt that the "atmosphere" in the darkness was the breath of the Holy Spirit as John said. In that atmosphere, at times, I sensed God filling and containing all things, but I could not feel it. I thought that God was filling me with grace as He contains me in the Darkness. It was painful. But I also felt that the pain I experienced was the death pains of my false self, and at the same time, the birth pains of true self.

Then one night in prayer: God goes before me preparing everything by being in everything that is and that happens. Mary holds my hand and leads me along the way. The Way, the Truth, and the Life is Jesus. As I was led to others, I could see Jesus Forsaken in the faces of each person. Everyone in this world suffers in some way, even if they do not know it. Jesus said, "Be at peace in all situations. Everything works together for your good." He said that my life right now is like a cloth being wrung out. You start at one end and work to the other ... from past to present. As God squeezes the painful memories out, you remember and feel them. This squeezing process is painful but makes my life new. Jesus is the way I am going, the truth I am now seeing, and the life to which I am going. New wine skins for new life in them! Along this way, I began to feel that I was beginning to understand myself and the world better. It reminded me of Katagiri Roshi telling me: "Take each step knowing that you are always stepping on the back of a Water Buffalo." It is like God is there under each step you take. "Courage. It is I. Do not be afraid." (Mk 6:50)

One day, it seemed like Jesus was with me looking at the boy in the box. There was a hole in the boy's heart full of worms from the painful past. In that hole, the Cross was planted with Jesus on it. Jesus Forsaken makes himself one with the boy, with me, with everyone since all humans suffer. The boy in the box moves and Jesus Forsaken moves with him: one movement of pain both human and divine. I realized that if I embrace the boy in the box, myself in the box, all persons in their boxes, I embrace Jesus. Jesus beside me said, "Look at the wounds I still carry in My body. So, you will also carry wounds with you ... in your body." I responded, "But I can barely function." He responded, "You will be able to function just as I am able to function with all the wounds I carry." Jesus was sitting next to me, and we embraced each other with a boy suffering in a box with Jesus on the Cross in the worm hole. Jesus said to me, "Accept your wounds as Me forsaken, and with Me we will travel together on the way our Father has planned for us."

CHAPTER 21

Humankind and Nature

As time went on, it seemed more and more like I could see things in a new and more loving way. I went to Mass at St. Anselm Church, an African American Catholic Church on the South Side of Chicago. Looking at the people there, whom I had seen at other times, they now seemed like precious children of God. Also, I went to the Art Institute, and there was a photo display of homeless people in Chicago. Looking at them, I felt not only a kinship with them but also a calling to something having to do with them. I will say more about this calling in the Epilogue.

Also, I began to feel a foretaste of unity with humankind and nature. John writes about both kinds of unity that happens after the dark night of the spirit. Concerning unity with humankind, John writes, "The Father loves them by communicating to them the same love He communicates to the Son ... that they be so [united] through the union of love, just as the Father and the Son are one in unity of love." (CB 39. 5) Concerning nature, John writes, "[God] nurtures and gives being to all creatures rooted and living in Him ... shows Himself to her [nature] and reveals

Himself as Creator.... The knowledge of this harmony fascinates and delights the soul." (CB 39.11)

I would add that what John writes about unity and love remind me of the charism of love and unity in the Focolare spirituality. John saw these graces as aspects of union with God in the sixteenth century. Chiara received her charism in the twentieth century. The dark night of the spirit enabled John to live his spiritualty in union with God. My Dark Night enabled me to live my spirituality of love and unity toward the ideal of a united world today. I am forever grateful to John for guidance through my Dark Night.

I shared my coming out of the Dark Night with Masao Abe. He said, "This might be the beginning of the awakening of your True Self. You cannot awaken to your True Self. It has to awaken in you and become your new life." I remembered that months ago, Jesus said to me: "You are afraid to live your life." Now, I am beginning to feel I can. And I am getting glimpses of what this new life entails. I wrote, "I am moved to forget myself ... to spontaneously care for humanity and nature in each moment with self-forgetfulness."

One night in a prayer experience, I felt God with me showing me all sorts of things from flowers to people. I felt I could love and enjoy all the things He showed me in a new and bright light. I remember in that experience seeing Jesus going out of the cave, standing risen. Reflecting on this later, I thought that during these recent months I have been coming out of a dark cave into the light of day ... risen from the Dark Night.

Some days later, I was helping in the nursery at a retreat. I thought that these little children, some were even babies, were pure. They had not formed false selves. I could see God/Love in them. I loved them. We played and it was wonderful. I discovered that I could take them each into my heart. I sensed the children felt it too as they crawled to me and climbed on me.

At Mass, I sat next to a 12-year-old girl, and she felt like my daughter. At the games in the afternoon, I was with an eight-year-old boy, and again, I felt my heart opened up to him. On the last evening, a young girl sang a song about Mary. It made me feel like Mary was my mother loving me in this girl. It was a very strong grace that led to tears and shaking. I thought that by the grace of God, I was now able to bring others in my heart as Mary contains me in her heart. The Light that created the Darkness in which I have been living is now shining on the world around me, and I am discovering a world to be loved. I now feel a freedom to love and fill my heart with others like a small Mary.

At the last Mass, I could "feel" Jesus in all of us. I realized that that what I do to others, I do to Him. Jesus in us links us all as brothers and sisters in the family of God. I also saw that I am like everyone else. We all are humans, and so we are all flawed, suffer, and struggle. We all carry our crosses, even those who do not know it. This gave me a new sense of solidarity with other people. Then there was the Eucharist! Jesus becomes food from Paradise giving us the life of Paradise to live on earth!

The love I have found emerging from my "cell" is not an act of the will, but an overflowing from the heart. The source of the flow is God. There are no words to describe the size of God. I see that He makes Himself so tiny that He is not only in humans, but in even the ants and grains of sand. He is also so large that He is universally under all creation, weaving all creatures together in a tapestry of life and love, or as notes in a cosmic symphony. It is surprising that I see this. Another surprise is that when I focus on God alone and nothing else, it seems like everything is my brother or sister.

CHAPTER 22

Opening Up

I have come to feel deeply that God is asking me to begin to put down my emotional barriers now that I have more of a sense of my true self, and to relate to others with more of an emotional connection. I was not sure what this meant since I had already been able to love others more than ever in the past. Then one night, I dreamt that I was at a meeting with some Jewish survivors of the Holocaust. They were silent. I asked them why they were silent. They did not answer. When I awoke, I realized that for years I have been facing some terrible and painful things in the Darkness. Now, as the Darkness lifts, I am tired due to what has happened to me and sad about what I have seen. I feel the need for some time to process and heal. But, God wants me to take down emotional barriers and focus on connecting more with other people. I remembered Jesus saying, "Pick up your cross and follow Me." I sensed that God may be calling me to put down emotional barriers. It is true that I have always kept an emotional distance from people. Ann was the first person I trusted enough to put down my emotional barriers. Now, God is asking me to do this with everyone.

Then, I read about a charismatic healing Mass in Indianapolis. I had learned about the charismatic experience in the Church from Don Gelpi at the Jesuit School of Theology and was surprised and impressed. That night, I had a dream that Barbara, my sister who had died, came to me and said I should go to that healing Mass. So, I drove down to attend. The priest truly had the gift of healing. I was impressed with the physical healings and the fact that not all who were healed were very religious. As I sat there, I prayed for the ability for put down my emotional barriers. I sensed the atmosphere of the Holy Spirit, and I felt a weight being removed from me. It was like a weight I could not let go of by myself, and it was taken by the Holy Spirit.

The next day, Ann and I helped friends move into a new house. I felt "normal" and "free." I worked all day and was fine. I also had a full range of feelings ... being concerned about Kristy's living situation at Northwestern to an argument I had with Ann. As time went on, I did feel a bit adrift. This freedom seemed a bit too much. And I felt the desire to close down. But, I chose not to and when I did that, I felt peace again. Later, I wrote:

Springtime everywhere! God fills me with a new energy and binds me to Him and others in a new way! Release-ment, lightness, freedom, openness! I still have all my feelings, but now they flow more easily.

I felt like I was moving out of the Dark Night. At Mass, we heard the story of Abraham reaching the promised land. I feel like I too have been on a long journey to a kind of promised land. I prayed:

Jesus, you are the Light or the Fire within me. I feel now at one with you in the depths of my soul below the Darkness that has given me the wisdom to see my past and present as they truly are. This Light has come from You risen within me. But, I received it in the Darkness and pain where You made Yourself one with me in Jesus Forsaken. I feel one, in union, with You. And You have given me Yourself Forsaken as my spouse. My cross, darkness, and pain were what You took upon Yourself on Your Cross when You cried out, "My God, my God, why have you forsaken me." And then, "Into your hands I commend my spirit." So, with Jesus Forsaken, I put my spirit in God's hands so I can be raised to beyond my burial clothing to the fuller life in God's grace ... a taste of Paradise. Amen.

As time went on, I found myself to be more sensitive to the pain of others and more moved from deep inside to stop and reach out to them with love. As for what John said about unity with humankind, once in Chicago, I met a woman who was getting up from sleeping in a parking garage where Ann and I parked our car. I walked with her and asked her questions about what she called her "business," namely begging on the streets. She explained that each day, she would go to work on a certain block on Michigan Avenue and beg. From the money she received, she could take care of herself for a day or sometimes even a few days. So, when I would go to Chicago, I would always walk up to persons begging on the street, look them straight in the eyes, and ask how business was that day. They would look at me with surprise and then talk to me about their business. I would always give them money and wish them a good day. They always said, "Thank you."

As for what John said about nature, I would often take walks in the countryside near where I live. When I saw animals, even worms and ants, I would see all of nature expressing itself in them. They are gifts from God in the "grove," to use John's term, to be loved and cared for. All living and inanimate beings are unique and yet not separate. There is a deep unity that binds us all in God's love. This reminded me of when His Holiness the Dalai Lama said to me: "The way you treat any living being affects how you treat all living beings." The love of God shines in all things. All is in each and each is in all. The Glory of the Trinity is even in the dust and the stones. This was a glimpse at the new life I found outside the cell.

When I now turn my attention to Jesus Forsaken in myself, there is just He and me alone. I feel Him but do not see Him, just His presence in silence. In that silence, there is nothing to do, only to be ... not to be this or that ... but just be. He is a silent and secret love to which I surrender myself. When I look outside myself, what should I do? Just put love in each present moment so through me He can love all living beings. He fills my eyes with love and moves my body to reach out and love concretely.

I asked Masao Abe about suffering and enlightenment in Buddhism. He said that we are always in *samsara*, the world of suffering within and without. It is endless. But as our True Self awakens within, we find a Source for living compassion for others, each being we meet. This is the paradox: our Original Self is untouched and at the same time fully identified with our ordinary self in samsara. The Original Self is like water and the ordinary self is like waves on the water. This reminded me of what the Zen scholar Geshin Tokiwa said to me once in Japan: "Awakening to your True Self enables you to live ordinary self at the service of others. You still suffer, but suffering with others who suffer. This is the Great Compassion."

One evening, I sensed Jesus holding my shoulder and leading me to a garden with buildings around it. I was walking around the hallways of the buildings, looking from time to time into the central garden. When I finally entered, all noise stopped and there was stillness and clarity. Looking around, I saw many flowers and also many weeds. It was like looking into an inner garden in myself with flowers and weeds. An old gardener entered the garden with his tools. It seemed that Jesus was asking me to look at the old gardener in order to learn how to tend my inner garden. I thought the old gardener would dig up the weeds. But instead, he dug below the surface to an underground water source. This water source flows from the inner garden with its weeds and flowers to outside where it flows to the inner gardens of all humankind and all living beings. We will always have flowers and weeds in our inner gardens. But God is a deeper source of life-giving water that can reach all living beings. I am called now to be a gardener to open the inner water source of Love to all suffering beings, including myself. I said, "I can be who I truly am with both flowers and the weeds caring for others with their needs and limitations." We are all brothers and sisters linked by God with our flowers and weeds, in the garden of creation kept alive by an underground water Source.

A few months later, Ann and I were in the jungle outside Bangalore, India, at a Buddhist-Catholic dialogue sponsored by the Pontifical Council for Interreligious Dialogue. It was at a Benedictine monastery. One afternoon, I took a rest in the guesthouse. Outside were young girls carrying rocks to build a walkway. They were singing together—flowers! I saw the small village where they lived. No doors and dirt floors. But in that field of weeds, they were the flowers, loving each other from a Source deeper than the poverty.

In a flash of light in that jungle, God showed me that when I look at, listen to, or touch a person, he or she is Jesus for me in that moment. In this momentary light, I felt like the whole of creation was exploding with a sacredness. Seeing each person I meet in this way is the road ahead God is calling me to follow. And it is Jesus in me who sees Himself in others ... and I can feel that happening. And God is leaving me free to choose to love Him in my neighbor, in nature, and in even the rocks on a path. He leaves me free to let Him see my neighbor through my eyes. I find God in this dynamic, and that brings me joy, compassion, and love. This linkage in and through God brings us to the deep water Source in the garden that links us as one. May they all be one," as Jesus prayed. This reminds me of Dogen's saying, "Forget our self and we are enlightened by all beings."

CHAPTER 23

It's Simple:
Caring and Kindness,
Especially to the "Least"

A nn and I were at Mass in a poor part of San Francisco. We sat in the section for deaf people with a person who did sign language in front of us. There were a number of blind persons and also persons in wheelchairs. Some were mentally disabled. One young girl in a wheelchair moved her hair up and down and hit herself on the head with her other hand. Everything inside me stopped for the whole Mass, and I made no responses and did not sing the songs. At the handshake of peace, a woman in front of me say to me: "I was raised a Catholic girl and went to Catholic schools. But this is my first time back to Church." She was a street person who used a pen to write things during Mass. Her friend was an enraged young man from the streets. But he did nod at me and smile. I wanted to go over and shake the hand of the disabled girl who hit herself. I thought, *I also hit myself.* But God said to me: "Walk instead to the leper yourself." These words brought to mind St. Francis who was afraid of lepers and finally walked to one and kissed him.

Leaving Mass, I felt like the disabled and the helpers all blended into one. They care for each other, and in that mutual caring, they are one. I began sobbing uncontrollably as I felt I was in that one too. That is where I am meant to be—in that oneness of caring and kindness. We all had gone to receive God in the Eucharist. I need to receive all the suffering persons, and myself, in the oneness I experienced at that Mass ... the acceptance of the unacceptable with caring and kindness. Later, I thought that each person at the Mass is a child of God whom God loves and with whom Jesus Forsaken makes Himself one in their everyday conditions. I felt called to that oneness with all the broken parts of humanity.

Some weeks later, I was at another Mass. This one was at the National Shrine of the Immaculate Conception where Chiara was being honored. I felt a peace washing over me and felt like Chiara was my mother—a caring and kind mother of peace. At the Mass, I felt Jesus Forsaken close to me and a deeper love for Him than ever before. He asked me: "Do you love me?" I said, "Yes." And he replied, "Then feed my sheep." I thought of the Mass in San Francisco.

Over the next weeks and months, I felt like God was finally asking me to "stop and rest." It was 1999, eight years since the dark night began. As I began to rest, I looked to the future, but at the same time, I felt an intense grief over what I was leaving behind. It is like when Jesus asked persons to follow Him, and they responded that they needed to do something related to their past life. Jesus said, "Let the dead bury the dead." And in Isaiah: "Remember not the events of the past.... See, I am doing something new." (Is 43: 18–19) I wonder about the future ... I will just have to wait and see.

CHAPTER 24

Family and Dialogue

As a married layperson, not a priest or a monk, let me share about how this Night affected my family. The first Dark Night was light compared to this night. Also, we had three children who were very young. Ann and I were able to save them from any worry about me due to the fact that the Night was not so dark, and I was able to function well as a father. However, the second Dark Night was, as John writes, "like Hell." I could not function as I did during the first Dark Night, and it did affect Ann and the children who were still at home.

At the time the second Dark Night began in 1991, my eldest son Jim had graduated from Purdue University and was working in Chicago. Also, my daughter Kristy was at Northwestern. During this Night, Jim would move to Los Angeles and Kristy would move to Boston. When I saw them, I could bring myself to seem like I was fine. However, this was not the case with Ann and my sons David and Paul. I asked them to share what it was like for them during the eight years of the Second Night.

Ann

Don and I have been married for 53 years, raised four amazing children, and now have seven beautiful grandchildren. These years have been blessed with many joys, beautiful family memories, enjoyable adventures traveling to other countries, wonderful celebrations of educational, professional, and personal accomplishments, births, weddings, anniversaries, yearly family reunions at our home, and enough love to fill all of our hearts with warmth and gratitude. However, during the 1990s, Don seemed to be depressed, anxious, and fearful most of the time. He was always a loving father to our children, and I knew that he loved me as I loved him. But, during this time, he was frequently emotionally distant from me, as he became very focused on his own mental and emotional condition. He was also very dependent on me to be the major caregiver of our children and to support his emotional fragility. Don never really spoke to me about experiencing a spiritual Dark Night during the 1990s.

But, I was aware of his struggle for a deeper relationship with God. His struggle often caused difficulties for our relationship as husband and wife. I often felt as though I had another person to take care of rather than a spouse who could equally share the tasks of parenting and being a couple. Don, me, and our children strove to live the Focolare spirituality of love and unity in our daily lives. This was a tremendous help for me as I became the emotionally stable center of unity for our growing family.

David

When I was in college, in 1992, I lived at home for a year to save money so I could do some traveling in Europe. I remember one night that I heard my father and mother talking in their bedroom. My father said, "I hate being like this!" I felt sad that he was feeling that way, and I was afraid for him. My mother said that it was a phase and not permanent. His struggle was hard for all three of us. On the other hand, he always supported and encouraged me. When I needed him, he would always talk to and help me with what I needed. He was fully present when talking to me and never said he was feeling bad and had to go to his room. I expressed my love for him, and he expressed his love for me. When I moved to Charlotte, North Carolina, in 1993, he talked on the phone with me many times about being a first-year teacher in a tough school, and we had a wonderful relationship. The times he was the best was when we went to the Mitchell cabin on a lake in the mountains in Idaho to be with our relatives in 1993 and 1994. Also, a very important moment came in 1993. We were in San Diego visiting my grandmother and we went to the beach. When we arrived, he gathered us on the grass at a beachside park. He opened up about his struggle, and for all of us, it was a moment of deep love and family unity. This love and unity between us children continues to today. Then in 1995, he and my mother came to my wedding in Raleigh, North Carolina, and he acted like he was not struggling. I realized that his sadness would come and go. When he was not feeling well, he always helped from a distance. And when I came down with what turned out to be a chronic condition, he found a good doctor for me in Raleigh. Again, he was always supportive and encouraging, showing me that he loved me. And by 2000, he was over the sad times and was strong and healthy in mind and body.

Paul

I was born in 1980 and was the youngest of four children. The closest sibling in age to me was my sister Kristy who was nine years older. I recall doing things with my brothers Jim and David and my sister as well as my mother and father joining in their discussions. I had to mature quickly in order to feel like I was a part of the family. For this reason, I began having a more mature relationship with my father than most young children. It was as if my desire to be seen on the same level as my older siblings meant I needed to interact with him as an older child would. My father was someone to talk to, learn from, and even compete with in games and sports. As I grew, my father seemed to be quite active and happy to answer my endless questions about anything under the sun and to help me learn to play sports throughout the year—baseball, basketball, and most notably, tennis. Then, in the early to the late 1990s, I remember things changing in terms of my relationship with my father. It is important to point out that at this time, I do recall him becoming more detached. He was quiet and there seemed to be less joy in the house. While my father was always willing to grant my requests to practice a sport, drive me to a friend's house, or help me with a school assignment, he did so in a more melancholy manner. Then by 1999, I was in college, and I remember that he reviewed my papers and discussed topics from my social science classes with me with love and pride. By this time, when I came home or he came to Indiana University, it was clear that his joy in life had returned.

For myself, I was aware of how my condition affected Ann and our children. Ann was very concerned about what was happening to me. What she saw was me falling apart, often being isolated from her, and at times not being able to function at home. I would at times take long walks in the park, stay in my bedroom with the door closed, and feel depressed and lost in myself. Ann suffered from what was happening to me. And many times, she would have to make excuses for me to the children. I loved them deeply, and it was painful to experience a kind of distance from them. To this day, when I think about Ann and my children during those years, my heart breaks and I cry.

It seems that in the Dark Nights, a person can often function well at work. In fact, I was able to do my academic work at the university and also travel for dialogues with Buddhism. In fact, my work in dialogue included presentations at the 1993 Parliament of the World's Religions in Chicago where the Dalai Lama requested an intermonastic dialogue at Gethsemani Abbey, the home of his friend Thomas Merton. I was asked by the monastics, since I had worked with the Vatican's Pontifical Council for Interreligious Dialogue since 1986, to help then organize what came to be called "The Gethsemani Encounter" and to deliver the Christian opening address in 1996 ... which I did. In the meantime, I was invited to give the opening address at the Vatican's first Buddhist-Christian dialogue held in Taiwan in 1995. There, I was also asked to write the final statement that defined the new step forward for the Church's dialogue with Buddhism. Then in 1998, I gave a paper at the Vatican's second Buddhist-Christian dialogue that was held in India. Actually, I did not feel I could go there by myself since the Dark Night was very strong, so I made a deal with Ann. If she went with me, we would stop in Ireland. She is Irish, so she agreed.

This second Dark Night gave me the strength I needed to shift my dialogue focus after 9/11 to peacebuilding projects with the Department of State. I was able to build a network of universities and Muslim organizations in the United States to carry out dangerous interfaith peacebuilding projects from 2004 to 2009 in Kyrgyzstan, Lebanon, Algeria, Southern Thailand, and Mindanao in the Philippines. All were successful, and our work in the Philippines contributed to the final peace agreement between the Philippine government and the Moro Islamic Liberation Front.

After 2009, I returned to working with the PCID, then led by Cardinal Jean-Louis Pierre Tauran. I began working with him on the new Buddhist-Catholic dialogues of fraternity that Pope Francis asked for in order to focus on becoming "brothers and sisters" working together locally to local social issues. I was asked to lead the dialogue of action in the United States that has resulted in green affordable housing projects in Brooklyn, and hopefully also in Chicago, and Los Angeles. The housing is for homeless men, couples, and women with children. All of these projects with Muslims and Buddhists were opportunities for me to do the will of God for me that I learned from the Dark Nights: Caring and Kindness, especially to the "Least."

Finally, I want to thank Fr. James Connor, O.C.S.O; Keith Egan, T.O.C.; Fr. Brian O. McDermott, S.J.; Sr. Constance Fitz-Gerald, O.C.D; Fr. José Damián Gaián de Rojos, O.C.D.; and Fr. Piero Coda for their support and guidance in writing this book.